INTERCESSIONS AT THE PARISH COMMUNION

(following the Sunday themes in The
Alternative Service Book 1980: Years 1 and 2)

William C. Collins

MOWBRAY
LONDON & OXFORD

By the same author:

Introductions to the ASB Readings

Introductions to the Readings at Holy Communion
    (ASB) Year One
    (ASB) Year Two

Copyright © William C. Collins 1985

ISBN 0 264 66930 4

First published 1985
by A. R. Mowbray & Co. Ltd,
Saint Thomas House, Becket Street,
Oxford, OX1 1SJ

Phototypeset by Cotswold Typesetting Ltd, Gloucester
Printed in Great Britain by Richard Clay (The Chaucer Press)
Ltd, Bungay, Suffolk

ACKNOWLEDGEMENT
An extract from The Alternative Service Book 1980 is reproduced by kind
permission of the Central Board of Finance of the Church of England.

FOREWORD

The Eucharist is a door opened on heaven through which we can all enter. We make our prayer to God as much by what we do as what we say; as much by our silences as by our speech. The action is, in the first place, the act of God through Jesus our Lord, for ever offering the 'one oblation of himself once offered', and all we give we give through him and in him.

What we offer is 'ourselves, our souls and bodies', not merely ours alone, but all the particular people and things which are the daily concern of our lives. Our intercessions.

Intercession is not the poor relation of prayer, though it is sometimes treated like that. Nothing can replace the silent, speechless, adoration of God, and that precious silence is, for many people, an oasis of spiritual strength to which they return repeatedly in Communion. Compared with the consciousness of God speaking to us, our own putting into words of our all-too-human hopes, needs and gratitude can seem all too feeble.

Yet we know that in the exchange of love which is at the heart of God, 'He ever liveth to make intercession for us'. Our intercession can be one with the prayer of Jesus. And so it gives me pleasure to commend again the thoughtful and prayerful work of Bill Collins who has once again enriched our approach to really praying the Eucharist. It should be of the greatest help in stimulating a new depth and variety of loving prayer from us in response to that love with which he first loved us—the very heart of the Eucharist offering.

+ Michael St Germans

PREFACE

To pray is difficult; to write prayers even more so. For in a very real sense, written prayers, whether they be private or intercessory, represent a fundamental contradiction in terms. The most effective, potent and spontaneous prayers are often inarticulate, or at best grammatically awkward. A prayer is often an incomplete sentence, a sigh, an exclamation, a word, or perhaps even an unexpressed thought or wish. More often than not, prayer is spoken from the heart, not formulated on paper, and therefore any attempt to capture this spontaneity in the written word is bound to fall short of the ideal.

However, as intercessory prayer is an integral part of the Sunday liturgy in so many churches today, it seemed helpful that a set of examples should be made available for the laity to use, or adapt to its own particular circumstances. The prayers follow the pattern of the Sunday themes suggested by the ASB lectionary and fit easily and naturally into the structure of the liturgical rites.

In writing these prayers, several considerations and principles have shaped my approach to the task. The most important of these principles is a realization that the most effective intercessory prayer is self-effacing. It is prayer in which the intercessor remains virtually anonymous: functioning merely as a representative of the worshipping community, a channel through which petitions on behalf of particular concerns are laid at God's feet for his consideration as he sees fit, and without conditions, manipulation, or personal intervention. This is not to say that Intercessions may not reveal attitudes and feelings in connection with those concerns and needs which they identify. It is merely a reminder that when it comes to intercessory prayer, God is in charge, his will be done, and we who make our petitions must be ready and willing to accept, reinforce, and co-operate with that will. A recognition of this important premise will prevent us from asking God to respond to problems for which we are unwilling to accept the responsibility. God cannot be expected to create harmony in a situation concerning which, by our own behaviour, we promote discord. No one would deny that there can be no absolution without confession, no conversion without repentance. In the same way, it is imperative that we understand that intercessory prayer must incorporate not only a petition in the faith that God will respond, but also, and perhaps this is even more important, an acknowledgement of our personal responsibility to accept and act in accordance with his response, whatever it may be. As Christ's disciples, we may be expected to give assent to whatever answers God gives to our intercessions, and it is for this reason that we must maintain a position of relative flexibility, if not neutrality, so that God may use us to fulfil his will and purpose.

Another purely technical consideration in shaping the prayers of this collection emerges from my observation that many of the currently available published prayers are carried away by their own rhetoric. They appear contrived, stilted, and riven with cliches and ecclesiastical jargon. Such prayers may be suitable in the formal atmosphere of cathedral worship, but at the parish level they are too restrictive and simply out of place. I do not for one moment seek to minimize the dangers of falling into this pitfall; prayer is acutely vulnerable to the lure of rhetoric and jargon. Yet in the case of intercessory prayers, such as those of this collection, which are intended for parish use, it is essential to try and keep them short and concise, yet as natural and spontaneous as possible within the restrictions of the written word. Moreover, I have tried to incorporate sufficient flexibility to permit the inclusion of whatever specific petitions may be appropriate on a particular occasion. To this end there are frequent pauses within petitions to allow for such inclusions. With this provision, the intercessory prayers of this book are designed to be used in conjunction with the existing rubrics of The Alternative Service Book 1980.

INTERCESSIONS AT THE PARISH COMMUNION
for use at the Alternative Services

(Fifth Sunday before Advent)

The Creation

For the Church:

> Lord, we bring before you the Church, your
> living body in all its strengths and weaknesses,
> successes and failures. . . . Create in us and all
> your people new attitudes, new hearts, that we
> may bear fresh and imaginative witness to the
> powers of your love.

For the world:

> Lord, the nations of this world are either poor
> and desperate or rich and selfish. There seem to
> be no bridges of concern between them. Create
> between the leaders of nations bonds of mutual
> sensitivity and compassion, a renewed awareness
> of their common humanity, that the world may
> be healed by the power of your peace and
> reconciliation.

For the local community:

> Lord, we lay before you our local community, its
> families and institutions. Look upon our
> relationships in love, healing our divisions and the
> conflicts which divide us. . . . Create in us an
> awareness of your compassion, the will to be
> tolerant of others, and the imagination to realize
> that reconciliation is born of an understanding
> both of self and of others.

For those in need:

Lord, behold the sick and the poor, the lonely and the oppressed, those who are crippled by despair and poisoned with bitterness. In their need they wait to be made whole, to be created new in the light of your healing power . . .

For those who have died:

Lord, we bring before you those who have died, and those who are on the threshold of death. . . . May they discover in the cross of Christ the courage to look beyond its burden, a reminder that to die is to be newly born, newly created in your kingdom, and the confidence to believe that death is but a door to new life in your presence.

Finally . . .

Rejoicing in the fellowship of (N and of) all your saints, we commend ourselves and all Christian people to your unfailing love.

(Fourth Sunday before Advent)

The Fall

For the Church:

> Lord, we lay before you the Church, and its
> leaders. . . . We confess a distorted view of your
> will, a weakness of faith, a lack of imagination to
> respond positively and creatively to our calling as
> disciples in a rapidly changing world. By our
> sectarian strife, our mutual fears and suspicions,
> we fall away from your grace and favour. We are
> unlovable, Lord, yet you persist in loving us. Heal
> our divisions, Lord; make us whole.

For the world:

> Lord, we pray for a sinful and brutal world, a
> world in which nations and governments are all
> too often ruled by the passions of ambition,
> greed, deceit, and corruption, a world scarred by
> the wounds of man's inhumanity to man. . . . Yet,
> fallen as we are, we are your creation, Lord. By
> your creating will may we stand again and
> flourish.

For the local community:

> Lord, we pray for the families of our parish and
> community. . . . Too often our homes become
> prisons, cutting us off from neighbour and
> stranger. Remind us, Lord, that only by loving

and reaching out to others can we love and reach out to you; only by denying ourselves, can we find ourselves.

For those in need:

Lord, we lay before you the sick and the poor, the despised and the rejected. . . . We confess that we care too little and too late for them, that in the flush of our own health and prosperity they are too easily forgotten and passed by. Yet the Samaritan chides us, while the poor and the meek await their inheritance of your kingdom. Make us mindful, Lord.

For those who have died:

We pray for those who have died. We pray that you will receive them in love. . . . For them, what was once obscure is now clear, once hidden now revealed, once in darkness now set in the perpetual light of your mercy and forgiveness. Once they were fallen, Lord. Now, by your grace, let them stand in your kingdom.

Finally . . .

Rejoicing in the fellowship of (N and of) all your saints, we commend ourselves and all Christian people to your unfailing love.

(Third Sunday before Advent)

The Election of God's People, Abraham

For the Church:

> Lord, we offer prayers for your Church, its clergy
> and people . . . As members of your living body,
> elected to preach love in the midst of a loveless
> world, we pray for the insight to know your will
> for us, and the faith, wisdom, and courage to
> respond accordingly.

For the world:

> We pray for nations and governments, for
> political institutions appointed to make policy,
> keep order, and promote social justice in a
> troubled and divided world . . . In a world
> plagued by mediocre standards of leadership, raise
> up men of vision and imagination, statesmen
> whose programmes and policies will be a direct
> reflection of your compassion and reconciliation.

For the local community:

> We lay before you our community, its families
> and institutions . . . Especially we pray for
> parents – for mothers and fathers – whom you
> elect to receive the blessing and responsibility of
> raising children in the image of your love. give
> them the courage, faith, and humility to seek the
> strength and wisdom for their task in you.

For those in need:

And now we turn our thoughts to any of your children who are in need — the sick and lonely, the poor and the oppressed . . . Lord, we know that some of us are elected to suffer more than others; to be frail while our neighbour is robust, to live alone, whereas we would choose company. Our only comfort is the certainty that in our affliction, we follow in the steps of our Lord, that he will not desert us, and that his kingdom is our reward.

For those who have died:

We remember those who have died, those whose appointed time has come . . . May the memories they leave, the faith they have kindled in our hearts, be an inspiration to our own witness as God's chosen disciples in our community.

Finally . . .

Rejoicing in the fellowship of (N and of) all your saints, we commend ourselves and all Christian people to your unfailing love.

(Second Sunday before Advent)

The Promise of Redemption: Moses

For the Church:

> We offer prayers for all members of Christ's
> living body, the Church, for its clergy and people
> ... We pray that as we approach the Advent
> season, we may be prepared to receive the
> promise of our redemption, the good news of
> God's coming in love into a world that has lost
> its spiritual identity.

For the world:

> Lord, we pray for a world redeemed by you in
> your Son, yet oblivious to its redemption. We lay
> before you nations caught up in the death of
> violence and hatred, ignorant of your promise to
> visit them with your offering of new life. May
> the noise of war cease, that your message of
> redemption may be heard, that your stubborn
> creation may hear and understand.

For the local community:

> Lord, we offer prayers for the families and citizens
> of our local community, and for officials to whom
> is entrusted the stewardship of our resources and
> common welfare ... May they work together to
> build a community in which our Lord's infinite
> love for even the least of mankind is mirrored in
> our mutual concern for one another.

For those in need:

> We pray for the sick; for those who are afflicted in mind and body, those who are oppressed, frightened, and exploited . . . May they hear in their suffering the loud and clear voice of your comfort, the message of their redemption.

For those who have died:

> We offer prayers for the souls of those whose earthly lives are over, and whose risen life has begun . . . In them your promise of salvation is fulfilled; in the example of faith which they have left us, the confidence in our own resurrection is strengthened.

Finally . . .

> Rejoicing in the fellowship of (N and of) all your saints, we commend ourselves and all Christian people to your unfailing love.

FIFTH SUNDAY
BEFORE CHRISTMAS
(The Sunday before Advent)

The Remnant of Israel

For the Church:

> Lord, we offer you the Church, that portion of
> your creation whose faith keeps your love alive
> in the world . . . Bless your living body with the
> wisdom and insight to worship you in faith, the
> courage and conviction to follow you in hope,
> and the humility to accept you in love.

For the world:

> We pray for the world; for nations to whom
> your redeeming love will soon be revealed . . .
> Raise up leaders of stature to serve you in their
> stewardship of the world's resources. Prepare their
> hearts to receive you in trust and humility, that
> the policies which they enact may be established
> in the spirit of compassion, reconciliation, and the
> common good.

For the local community:

> Lord, we bring before you the families and
> institutions of our local community . . . As the
> parish church of . . . we are a remnant of faith
> chosen to serve you, called upon to personify
> your love among friends and neighbours, to
> preach your gospel in our daily life. Assist us,
> Lord; sustain us in our witness.

For those in need:

>We pray for the needy and the oppressed, for the sick and the poor, for that portion of your people called upon to suffer in your service, and in the image of your Son's passion . . . Grant to them courage and dignity in all that they must endure, that they may follow their blessed Lord into the peace of your kingdom.

For those who have died:

>Lord, we remember those who have died in faith and now live with you in your kingdom . . . In them we have borne witness to the dignity of death and the absolute certainty of resurrection. We thank you for the inspiration of their faith and courage, and we pray for the strength to follow their example when the time for our own departure draws near.

Finally . . .

>Rejoicing in the fellowship of (N and of) all your saints, we commend ourselves and all Christian people to your unfailing love.

(Fourth Sunday before Christmas)

The Advent Hope

For the Church:

> Lord, we pray for a Church in disarray – a
> Church divided in its mission and confused in its
> purpose . . . As your living body we are
> wounded, Lord. We are sick with faithlessness
> and we await the coming of your healing power,
> your capacity to revitalize our life with courage,
> faith, and singleness of purpose. Come quickly,
> Lord.

For the world:

> Dear God, we lay before you the nations of this
> world – their governments, leaders, and people
> . . . The world is stricken with terror, cowers in
> fear, as it is gradually consumed by the cancer of
> conflict and self-destruction. In the midst of our
> agony we hear your assurance of our deliverance,
> your Advent promise of our redemption. Visit us
> with your peace, Lord, that we may be saved
> from ourselves.

For the local community:

> We pray for our families, friends, and all who live
> and work in our local community . . . May your
> Advent promise of love, your spirit of hope and

reconciliation, bind us together, thereby enabling us to anticipate the future in confidence and the assurance of increased opportunities and prosperity.

For those in need:

Lord, we offer up to you the sick and the poor, the lonely and the frightened – those who suffer in mind and body. It is especially to them that God comes. To them the promise of salvation is made. May they discover in the Advent hope new resources or courage, comfort, and faith in the God who redeems them.

For those who have died:

We remember the departed, those whose hope in the resurrection has been realized . . . Having left the world and taken a place in your kingdom, they experience Advent as a promise kept, a life saved and renewed by your redemptive power. May we ultimately follow them to our own eternal glory.

Finally . . .

Rejoicing in the fellowship of (N and of) all your saints, we commend ourselves and all Christian people to your unfailing love.

The Word of God in the
Old Testament

For the Church:

> Lord we pray for ourselves as members of your
> living body, the Church. We pray for other
> Christian communities throughout the world . . .
> As ministers of your reconciliation in the world,
> we pray for the courage and faith to co-operate
> with you in our own renewal, that being united
> and strong, we may fulfil your best hopes for us
> and live up to our calling.

For the world:

> Father, we pray for nations and governments,
> especially those in which fundamental human
> rights are violated, and offences against humanity
> most despicable . . . May Advent be a season in
> which you remind us that your promise of
> redemption is universal, that your will to save
> encompasses all mankind.

For the local community:

> We pray for the families of our local community,
> families often in conflict and in need of your
> healing power . . . May they discover in your
> Advent promise the impetus for renewal, the
> basis of a new covenant relationship rooted in
> mutual trust, respect, and love.

For those in need:

Lord, we lay before you the poor and dispossessed, the homeless, the weak and the frightened, those who are sick in mind and body . . . Your covenant is with them, Lord. To them you make your promise of redemption in a very special way. Soon you will come into the community of suffering as the Christchild of love and comfort. Make us ready to receive you.

For those who have died:

We pray for the souls of the departed, those who now share the eternal life promised by God through his Son . . . May we perceive in the strength of their witness the assurance of our own reward, and may their example open our hearts to receive the promise of God's redemption.

Finally . . .

Rejoicing in the fellowship of (N and of) all your saints, we commend ourselves and all Christian people to your unfailing love.

The Forerunner

For the Church:

> Lord, we lay before you the Church, your living
> body sent out to proclaim your love in an
> unloving word. Each of us, as a member of the
> Christian community, is called upon to prepare
> your way, to be a forerunner of your return, and
> to bear witness to the reconciliation which you
> offer. Our mission is vital; lend us your strength.

For the world:

> We pray for a world in turmoil, for nations
> engaged in mortal combat. Into the midst of this
> struggle bursts John the Baptist with his call to
> repentance, his announcement of the kingdom at
> hand. May his commanding presence quench the
> hatred and greed that makes for conflict and
> suffering. May his message bring peace to the
> hearts of men and women . . .

For the local community:

> We offer you our community – our homes,
> schools, and businesses as they anticipate the
> Christmas season . . . Yet even as we delight in
> the decorations which herald the approaching
> festivities, we pray that in our commercial
> preparations we will not ignore the spiritual gift
> that is promised.

For those in need:

> We pray for those in need – the lonely, the sick, the oppressed. We have in mind those in whom pain and adversity would seem to herald only hopelessness and despair; those for whom Advent promises not hope, but rather increased futility and bitterness. Help them to perceive a ray of hope in the gloom that surrounds them, and let Isaiah's message of consolation be a beacon to lead them out of darkness and into the light . . .

For those who have died:

> We offer you the souls of those who have given up their earthly lives and have gone before us into the kingdom . . . As forerunners of our own resurrection, may their faith inspire us, and may we discover in their passing the way to our own redemption.

Finally . . .

> Rejoicing in the fellowship of (N and of) all your saints, we commend ourselves and all Christian people to your unfailing love.

ADVENT 4 Years 1 and 2
(The Sunday next before Christmas)

The Annunciation

For the Church:

> We pray for the Church – its bishops, clergy, and
> people . . . In the Christian community you
> announce to the world your presence in human
> affairs. As members of this community, we are the
> focus of your Holy Spirit at work in the world.
> May we be worthy of your trust and useful to
> your purpose.

For the world:

> Lord, we raise up to you a broken world in which
> your annunciation of love offers the assurance of
> reconciliation. May the din of conflict subside that
> the angel's song of peace may be heard. And
> may Mary's anticipation of motherhood be
> mirrored in your creation's confident expectation
> of renewal . . .

For the local community:

> We pray for our cities, villages, and towns – for
> our families as they make the final preparations
> for the Christmas festivities . . . Just as God
> employed Mary in his strategy for human
> redemption, so may he use our families to
> exemplify the peace and love that will be born in
> the Christchild.

18

For those in need:

Lord, we offer up to you the disadvantaged and dispossessed among your children – the deprived and the rejected. May the healing power announced to the world in the witness of your Son bring comfort and relief to those elected to suffer. And may the plight of those who have little inspire humility in the hearts of those who have much.

For those who have died:

Lord, we remember those whom death has taken from us, those who are at peace in your kingdom. Help us to realize that it is through their faith and witness that you speak to us who follow them. Bless us with the imagination and perception to hear you . . .

Finally . . .

Rejoicing in the fellowship of (*N* and of) all your saints, we commend ourselves and all Christian people to your unfailing love.

The Birth of Christ

For the Church:

> Lord, we offer prayers for the Church, that
> community of witnesses which is the living body
> of the child whose birth we celebrate . . . May
> the angel's song of peace be the Church's
> message of hope and confidence to a cynical and
> troubled world. And may the beauty of the
> Christchild be reflected in the light which the
> Church holds out to a lost and confused people.

For the world:

> Dear Lord, the whole world is summoned to the
> cradle of Bethlehem by a star. There is room for
> the whole of mankind to gather round the
> manger to see and feel the love that is born
> there. Could nations but lay down their arms
> long enough to be consumed by the love of the
> Christchild, they would never take them up
> again. Let it be so!

For the local community:

> We pray for our community, and especially our
> homes on this Christmas day. In many of them,
> the lights of Christmas reflect joyful faces, food
> and drink fuel festive spirits, and the music of
> carols proclaim Christmas joy. But in other homes
> there is darkness, hunger, and despair. Our prayer
> is for them.

For those in need:

Lord, we pray for the poor and the
oppressed – for those who are sick and disabled,
whose vulnerability is mirrored in the utter
dependence and vulnerability of the Christchild
. . . May we, as witnesses of God's love, work to
spread his compassion in the community of need
and suffering that surrounds us.

For those who have died:

As we celebrate the birth of God's love in the
world, we remember with a mixture of sorrow
and joy those who have died to the world, but
now live in the Spirit of the risen Christ. The
baby Jesus is born; loved ones depart. May we
who linger so nurture the love that the
Christchild brings, that when the time of our
departure comes we may leave a song of peace in
human hearts.

Finally . . .

Rejoicing in the fellowship of (N and of) all your
saints, we commend ourselves and all Christian
people to your unfailing love.

The Incarnation

For the Church:

> Lord, we offer you the Church, that community
> of faith in which your world has been born and is
> at work ... May your people be increasingly
> aware this Christmas season that there is only
> one song with the power to soothe hearts and
> change the life of humanity – the song of love.

For the world:

> Lord, in this Christmas season your voice
> struggles to assert itself and be heard above the
> clamour of global conflict. Your creation is broken
> and divided: at war with itself and diverted from
> the path of its true destiny under your creating
> power ... Lord, we pray that at this time of
> international crisis, your still small voice may
> prevail to save us from our own perversity and
> folly.

For the local community:

> Lord, your incarnate Son walks the streets of our
> local community. He sits in the classrooms of our
> schools, occupies the beds of our hospitals, and
> has a place at table in our homes. Open our eyes,
> Lord, that we may see him, our lips that we may
> praise him, and our hearts that we may receive
> him. May his love bind us together and make us
> whole.

For those in need:

Lord, we bring before you those who are ill,
poor, and frightened – those who are lost and
alone . . . May the Christmas season signify for
them the birth of hope and renewal through your
healing love. May you visit them in their
suffering and raise their faith to make them
whole. By the energy of your creating power
may you transform frailty into vitality, weakness
into strength.

For those who have died:

Lord, there are loved ones and friends whom we
have lost. They now live with you in your
kingdom and view our Christmas celebrations
from above. We believe that something of their
faith and goodness is born with you at Bethlehem
and informs our own lives and witness. Guide us,
Lord, that when our time to die approaches, we
may be reunited with them in your light and
peace.

Finally . . .

Rejoicing in the fellowship of (*N* and of) all your
saints, we commend ourselves and all Christian
people to your unfailing love.

The Holy Family

For the Church:

> Lord, we pray for the Church, your spiritual
> family in the world ... We are your children, and
> as our spiritual Father and Creator, you share all
> of the concerns and expectations of any parent:
> obedience to your will and the fulfilment of our
> potential as witnesses to your love. May we
> grow strong and healthy in the faith which you
> demand of us.

For the world:

> We offer prayers for the world and its
> governments, a family of nations in disarray, a
> community polluted by the poisons of greed,
> cynicism, and hatred ... As the father of
> mankind, you grieve at our self-inflicted crises;
> you mourn our rejection of brotherhood and
> mutual love, our blindness to the peace that you
> will for us. Discipline your family, Lord, that your
> will may be done.

For the local community:

> We pray for our community and its families,
> especially those families in which there is strife
> and dissention. We pray for children and parents
> who have lost communication with each other,

and between whom there is no longer that bond of trust and mutual respect vital to the health of family life. Visit them, Lord, in the healing power of your reconciliation.

For those in need:

We offer prayers for those in need – for the sick, the poor, and for those who fail to realize their full potential in society: those for whom life has become a wasteland of discouragement and desolation. Awake in them a renewed awareness of their importance as members of your spiritual family, and give them patience in their suffering.

For those who have died:

We remember those who have died, and have discovered the eternal rest and peace of life in your kingdom. We mourn their loss but rejoice in their reward. Our earthly family is the poorer for their absence; your kingdom the richer for their presence . . .

Finally . . .

Rejoicing in the fellowship of (*N* and of) all your saints, we commend ourselves and all Christian people to your unfailing love.

THE EPIPHANY OF OUR LORD Years 1 and 2
(6 January)

The Revelation of Christ to All Men

For the Church:

> We offer thanks for the Church, Christ's living
> body in which God reveals himself to the world
> ... We pray that our witness may demonstrate
> God's purpose so clearly that his love may shine
> ever more brightly in the surrounding darkness.

For the world:

> Lord, we pray for a discordant world – a world
> broken and in desperate need of enlightenment.
> Bless your creation with an acute awareness of
> your creating power. Open the eyes, hearts, and
> minds of those in authority that they may
> perceive the revelation of your love and use it in
> wielding the power which they possess.

For the local community:

> We offer you our community – our homes,
> institutions, families, and friends. We know that in
> community life you reveal the social dimension of
> your gospel: the good news of social
> interdependence, concern, and trust. Father, we
> pray for the wisdom and humility to hear your
> voice, and to efface ourselves as individuals, that
> the vitality and prosperity of our community may
> be maintained.

For those in need:

> Lord, we lay before you those who are ill and poor, those who are distressed and in need of love and compassion . . . Remind us that the primary purpose of your revelation is to heal the sick, to make whole and strong a broken humanity. Through the healing ministry of human agencies may you establish a very special relationship with the disadvantaged, the have-nots, of your creation.

For those who have died:

> We pray for those who have died, for the souls of those who now see you face to face in your kingdom . . . To them is given the fulness of your revelation, the clearest demonstration of your love, which we, who linger in the world, cannot imagine. Eternal rest grant unto them, O Lord . . .

Finally . . .

> Rejoicing in the fellowship of (*N* and of) all your saints, we commend ourselves and all Christian people to your unfailing love.

Revelation: the Baptism of Jesus

For the Church:

> We pray for the Church, for clergy and people
> joined together in Baptism to be witnesses of
> God's love in a troubled world . . . May the
> sacramental power of initiation instil in the
> Christian community a new and creative
> relationship with the world, that through its
> witness, the living body of Christ may be at
> work in human affairs.

For the world:

> Lord, we lay before you a soiled world in need of
> cleansing, a broken and divided humanity
> awaiting your regeneration. Nations attack each
> other in hatred; would that they were baptized in
> your love. Governments fight each other out of
> fear and suspicion; would that they were washed
> in your trust and compassion . . .

For the local community:

> We pray for our community with its schools,
> homes, and families . . . Initiate in us a renewed
> appreciation of community spirit, a realization
> that communal prosperity and health depends
> upon the sensitivity and compassion of
> individuals. Baptize us, Lord, with a heightened
> awareness of our identity and purpose in the
> scheme of your creation.

For those in need:

> Lord, we offer up to you those in need of your special sustenance – the weak and the oppressed, the sick and the poor, those who are exploited in our society . . . They come to be baptized in the power of your healing spirit, to be washed clean in the waters of your comfort and compassion. Visit them, Lord, with your healing presence, that they may draw upon the strength and courage of your love.

For those who have died:

> We remember those who have died, those baptized and alive in the spirit of our Lord's resurrection . . . We rejoice in their witness, and pray that we who follow their example may one day be initiated with them into the light and peace of external life.

Finally . . .

> Rejoicing in the fellowship of (N and of) all your saints, we commend ourselves and all Christian people to your unfailing love.

Revelation: the First Disciples

For the Church:

> Lord, we lay before you the Church, raised by
> you to be your disciple in the modern world. We
> pray for its leaders, clergy, and people . . . Called
> upon to bear witness to your love, may the
> Christian community be filled with faith and
> courage to stand up and be counted, to hold the
> light of your truth high in these dark and
> troubled times.

For the world:

> We pray for nations – for governments and
> leaders called upon to serve them. Grant to
> elected officials the wisdom to perceive a mutual
> interdependence between secular authority and
> the spiritual imperative. Enable them to realize
> that political power and spiritual discipleship must
> go hand in hand, each reinforcing the other . . .

For the local community:

> We consider our community – our homes,
> institutions, and all citizens in whom you reveal
> yourself in love. May all of us demonstrate your
> gospel of compassion and reconciliation in such a
> way that our relationships may reflect the
> spiritual depth and quality of our communal life.

For those in need:

> We pray for the sick and the poor, those whose
> lives are without direction and purpose.
> Especially, we pray for . . . In their example we
> witness a discipleship of patience, courage, and
> trust — qualities demonstrated to perfection in the
> life and suffering of our Lord Jesus Christ.

For those who have died:

> We remember the departed, those whom you
> have called home to live with you in your
> kingdom . . . In their lives of faith, they were
> disciples of your love; now in their resurrection,
> they attest to your glory.

Finally . . .

> Rejoicing in the fellowship of (N and of) all your
> saints, we commend ourselves and all Christian
> people to your unfailing love.

Revelation: Signs of Glory

For the Church:

>   Lord, we pray for the Church and its ministry, a
>   visible and living sign of your redeeming
>   presence in the world . . . It is to the Church that
>   you have entrusted the care and nourishment of
>   your gospel of love and reconciliation, and we
>   pray that you will continually supply her with the
>   perception and imagination to bring your light
>   into the dark recesses of human relationships.

For the world:

>   We offer up to you nations in conflict —
>   governments in desperate need of the capacity to
>   perceive and act upon the many signs of your
>   redeeming will. We pray that the harmony of
>   your healing love may break through the discord
>   of national and international strife, that mankind
>   may step back from the brink of self-destruction
>   and discover the strength of your renewing spirit.

For the local community:

>   We pray for families of our community, for
>   parents and children, husbands and wives, with all
>   their hopes and aspirations. Be present, Lord, in
>   our homes, and in the bonds of trust and mutual
>   respect that are vital to the health and vitality of
>   family life. Use our families as a sign of your
>   reconciling will . . .

For those in need:

> We offer prayers for those in need, those who are ill, impoverished, and enjoy few of the pleasures or opportunities of life. Use them as a sign of your suffering presence in the world. We pray also for those engaged in the vocation of healing – for hospitals, doctors and councillors, that they may provide continuing evidence of your compassion and concern for your creation.

For those who have died:

> We remember those who have died and are raised with Christ into eternal life . . . In the miracle of resurrection, we bear witness to the supreme sign of your glory: your triumph over death and your affirmation of life.

Finally . . .

> Rejoicing in the fellowship of (N and of) all your saints, we commend ourselves and all Christian people to your unfailing love.

Revelation: The New Temple

For the Church:

> Lord, we pray for the Church, the living body of God's grace and his holiness in a hostile and irreverent world. As members of Christ's living body, we are called upon to be ministers in this temple, to preach by word and deed the peace and reconciliation of Christ in a fractious and broken world, to be shepherds of a wayward and lost flock . . .

For the world:

> Lord, we offer you the temple of your world, created good, but spoiled by the scars of war and violence . . . Lord, we pray that you would renew in your creation the values of brotherhood and interdependence, that we may rediscover our common identity as members of one undivided family created and sustained by your love: children of one household who call you 'Father'.

For the local community:

> We raise up to you our local community – our families and homes . . . Lord, how often we forget that our homes are the temple in which you live, our families ministers ordained to serve you in love. Concerned as we are with individual pursuits, we fail to appreciate the truth that when we break bread together as a family, we are at

worship with you, sharing the symbols of your living presence, consuming the living bread which you offer us. Turn our minds and hearts to receive you, Lord. Nourish us with your love.

For those in need:

We pray for the poor and the homeless, for the sick and the anxious, for those the temple of whose body is in need of restored health and renewal . . . For the bitter we pray sweetness, the despairing, comfort, the pained, relief, and for the lonely, companionship.

For those who have died:

We remember the departed, those whose souls are at rest in the temple of God's kingdom . . . We give thanks for the example of faith they leave us, and we pray for the courage and commitment to follow in their path.

Finally . . .

Rejoicing in the fellowship of (*N* and of) all your saints, we commend ourselves and all Christian people to your unfailing love.

Revelation: The Wisdom of God

For the Church:

> Lord, we pray for the Church and its leaders . . .
> In your wisdom you established the Christian
> community to show love to the world. Through
> its long and turbulent history, the Church has
> been persecuted, broken, and divided; yet by
> your strength it stands as testimony to your
> creating power. Grant it courage to move
> forward in faith.

For the world:

> We pray for nations in the grip of incompetent
> and ruthless leaders, nations whose governments
> fail to tap the infinite resources of your wisdom.
> You stand ready to guide them, Lord, yet the
> vanity of power excludes you. Make those in
> authority wise in humility that they may put the
> welfare of their people above political ambition.

For the local community:

> Lord, in your wisdom you have created
> community life to draw out and develop the
> talents of individuals. We pray for our own
> community and those who contribute to its
> activities . . . May they discover within their
> individual spheres of influence hitherto untapped
> resources of your creating power.

For those in need:

We pray for the sick and the poor – for those whose needs are greater than our own and whose suffering evokes in us the wisdom of compassion. Within the suffering community, there are those whose patience irritates us because it exposes our own impulsiveness. Lord, may the misfortune of others be for us the key to forbearance and concern.

For those who have died:

Lord, we remember those who have died – those who have discovered the ultimate wisdom of victory in resurrection. We who remain await the same miracle, praying that we will be worthy of the sublime privilege of living with you in your kingdom . . .

Finally . . .

Rejoicing in the fellowship of (N and of) all your saints, we commend ourselves and all Christian people to your unfailing love.

Revelation: The Parables

For the Church:

> We pray for the Church, its leaders and people
> ... As the living body of our Lord, we are called
> to preach Christ, the word of God, the supreme
> parable of redemption. Help us to communicate
> the good news of God's love in a clear and
> compelling witness.

For the world:

> We lay before you a broken and divided world –
> a world vulnerable to despair and in desperate
> need of God's revelation. We especially consider
> nations for whom the parables of Christ have
> immediate and poignant meaning ... Speak to
> our divisions with the message of healing and
> reconciliation, that peace may indeed be born into
> the world.

For the local community:

> Lord, we offer you our community – our homes,
> businesses and schools. We pray that the dialogue
> between parents and children, employers and
> employees, teachers and students, may be one in
> which mutual understanding and trust is fostered.
> May our community be a vital living parable of
> unity and goodwill to set before others.

For those in need:

We pray for those who are in need, those to whom Christ offers his parable of healing in a very personal way. For each of them there is a good Samaritan to offer help and compassion. Open their hearts and minds to receive Christ's assurance of comfort, courage, and sustenance.

For those who have died:

We remember the souls of those who have died and now rejoice in the perfect dialogue of peace and rest with Christ in his father's kingdom . . . For them the struggle is over, and the reward of salvation received. May our faith be such as to lead us to the glory of our own resurrection and reunion with those who have gone before us.

Finally . . .

Rejoicing in the fellowship of (N and of) all your saints, we commend ourselves and all Christian people to your unfailing love.

Christ the Teacher

For the Church:

> Lord, we offer up to you the Church as the
> means by which you continue Christ's ministry to
> the world. With the gospel as its text, the
> Christian community is called upon to teach and
> exemplify Christ's love and peace in a struggling
> and violent world . . .

For the world:

> We pray for a world deafened by
> conflict – nations blinded by hatred and oblivious
> to the instruction of love in your gospel. We
> offer our prayers for a world seemingly confused
> between reconciliation and appeasement, between
> greatness of spirit and weakness of heart . . .
> Teach nations to trust their neighbours in a spirit
> of tolerance and understanding, to negotiate their
> differences in the spirit of goodwill.

For the local community:

> We lay before you our community and its people
> . . . We pray especially for our schools and
> colleges, the focus of education and all academic
> endeavour. Bind teachers and students together in
> the spirit of mutual respect and commitment, that
> your gifts of knowledge and industry may take
> root and flourish.

For those in need:

Lord, we pray for those in need: the sick and the poor, the estranged and the lonely . . . Instil in them the spirit of your comfort and healing power. Help us to realize that suffering is the teacher of humility; that another's affliction teaches us to appreciate more fully the blessing of our own relative prosperity.

For those who have died:

We remember those who have died – those whose passing is a clear reflection of our own mortality, whose death is a powerful lesson of human impermanence . . . Being instructed in our own frailty, may we commit our earthly time more fully to the demonstration of your love and reconciliation in our relationships with others.

Finally . . .

Rejoicing in the fellowship of (*N* and of) all your saints, we commend ourselves and all Christian people to your unfailing love.

EIGHTH SUNDAY
BEFORE EASTER

Christ the Healer

For the Church:

Lord, we lay before you the Church and its
leaders . . . We pray that as the living body of
Christ, we may practise his healing ministry in an
ailing world; that just as our Lord brought the
healing power of reconciliation into his earthly
relationships, so may we, the Church, work to
reconcile the many differences which divide
mankind.

For the world:

We pray for a world which has lost sight of its
creator, for nations and leaders divorced from the
healing power of your love . . . Teach those in
authority that wise and creative government is
that which heals divisions and demonstrates
concern for the health and welfare of its people.
The time for binding the wounds of humanity
grows short, Lord. Bless governments with the
compassion to be merciful in their power.

For the local community:

Lord, we offer prayers for our local community
. . . We pray especially for our hospitals and
surgeries, and for the doctors and nurses who
bring to them your healing ministry. We pray for

the healing of our cultural and racial divisions; for tolerance and respect in our communal relationships.

For those in need:

We pray for the disadvantaged and the dispossessed; for those who are cynical and without faith. And we are mindful that it is to these people that Christ brings his ministry of healing and reconciliation. It is to them that our Lord's gospel is preached in a very special way. May those in need become increasingly aware of Christ's healing presence, that in the midst of their suffering, they may be comforted . . .

For those who have died:

We remember the departed, those whose souls are at rest in your kingdom . . . Each of them has experienced the supreme act of healing in the gift of resurrection. May our own witness be inspired by the legacy of faith and commitment which they leave behind.

Finally . . .

Rejoicing in the fellowship of (*N* and of) all your saints, we commend ourselves and all Christian people to your unfailing love.

Christ the Friend of Sinners

For the Church:

> We pray for the Church, called upon to express
> Christ's sinlessness in a sinful world . . . Renew
> your creation with an awareness of its
> shortcomings, that the living body of your
> Church may respond with imagination and
> courage in its ministry of reconciliation.

For the world:

> We lay before you a sinful world — nations in
> the midst of conflict, and governments broken by
> the forces of greed, fear, and hatred in the pursuit
> of self interest . . . Unaware of their need for
> redemption, they persevere in their folly. Lord,
> turn the attention of nations away from
> themselves, and make them more sensitive to
> others: more aware of their responsibility as
> members of a global community.

For the local community:

> Lord, we pray for our community – our homes,
> businesses, and schools. We acknowledge our
> shortcomings as citizens of . . ., our failure to
> make a full contribution to its life. Renew our
> commitment to the enrichment of community
> relations, and make our contributions worthy in
> your sight.

For those in need:

> We remember those in need . . . We acknowledge
> the important contributions of spiritual poverty,
> of sin, to human need and despair. We realize
> that physical disease is often but a symptom of
> spiritual decay. Visit the needy with spiritual
> renewal, that, their souls having been healed, they
> may better come to terms with their suffering.

For those who have died:

> We pray for those who have died, and must now
> answer to you for their sinfulness . . . We trust
> that mindful of their many demonstrations of faith
> and goodness, you will not now turn them away
> from your kingdom, and that when our time
> comes to stand before you, you will offer to us
> an equal portion of your love and compassion.

Finally . . .

> Rejoicing in the fellowship of (N and of) all your
> saints, we commend ourselves and all Christian
> people to your unfailing love.

The King and the Kingdom: Temptation

For the Church:

> Lord, we lay before you your Church, called to
> live and exemplify your gospel of love in an
> unloving world, to preach reconciliation in an
> atmosphere of seemingly irreconcilable tensions.
> How tempting it is for the Church to compromise
> the gospel for the sake of acceptability, to
> forsake its spiritual identity for political
> expediency, to be all things to all men. For the
> Church there is no easy way. Strengthen her,
> Lord.

For the world:

> Lord, we pray for a world caught in the unstable
> grip of temptation – for nations seduced by the
> forces of tyranny, greed, and selfish ambition . . .
> Caught up in the lust for power, governments
> lose sight of their commitment to serve, to look
> outward and seek the common good, the welfare
> and prosperity of their people. Lord, we pray for
> leaders of vision, courage, and spiritual greatness,
> who can resist temptation and work to bring
> peace and contentment to mankind.

For the local community:

> Lord, we bring before you our community . . .
> How tempting it is to look inward upon
> ourselves and our needs, to ignore our neighbour
> in favour of our own personal concerns, to isolate

ourselves from the community at large. Teach us
Lord that we are but members of a larger family.
Help us to see that input from without is vital to
the strength of our output from within.

For those in need:

We pray for the disadvantaged among us, those
who are ill, poor, and lonely . . . We recognize
the strong temptation they must feel to lapse into
a destructive state of bitterness and self-pity, and
we pray they be given the blessing of courage
and serenity to endure their affliction.

For those who have died:

We pray for the departed – those who have ~~traded~~ Exchanged
the temptations of earthly life for the
contentment and peace of your kingdom.
Liberated by our Lord's own suffering, death, and
resurrection, may we follow him and the faithful
departed into the peace that awaits us.

Finally . . .

Rejoicing in the fellowship of (N and of) all your
saints, we commend ourselves and all Christian
people to your unfailing love.

The King and the Kingdom: Conflict

For the Church:

We pray for the Church, its leaders and people
. . . Being mindful of the early Church's capacity
to endure and prosper in the face of persecution
and hostility, we pray that our own Christian
community, being vulnerable to the violence and
conflict in our modern world, may find in you the
courage to stand and be strong in your abiding
love.

For the world:

We lay before you a world scarred by conflict,
broken by man's inhumanity and greed . . . You
create us good, and we pervert your goodness.
You will us to love, and we clash in hatred. Do
not forsake us, Lord. Turn our hearts and make us
whole.

For the local community:

We pray for our community . . . We recognize a
persistent element of conflict and tension in our
relationships, and we confess to divisions which
threaten to disrupt and break down the fabric of
our communal life. Visit us, Lord, with your spirit
of reconciliation.

For those in need:

We offer you those whose need is great — those who are sick, poor, lonely, frightened, and lost ... We recognize in them the disharmony between mind and body, the conflict between spirit and flesh, and we pray for the harmony of your healing spirit to reconcile their conflicts and restore them to health.

For those who have died:

We remember those who have died, those who have given up the conflict of earthly life for the peace of your kingdom ... We thank you for their faith and loyalty to the good news which you proclaim, and we pray for the courage to build upon the example they have set us.

Finally ...

Rejoicing in the fellowship of (N and of) all your saints, we commend ourselves and all Christian people to your unfailing love.

The King and the Kingdom: Suffering

For the Church:

> We lay before you the Church: its leaders and
> people . . . We pray especially for the Christian
> community called upon to be Christ in the midst
> of hostility and persecution: the Church called
> upon to suffer at the hand of ruthlessness and
> aggression for the sake of the gospel . . . Grant
> to your disciples of suffering the courage to
> display that same outpouring of love and peace
> that your Son radiated from the agony of the
> cross.

For the world:

> We pray for a suffering humanity, nations in the
> grip of self-imposed torment and conflict. The
> spirit of man is under siege: his instinct of
> brotherly love threatened by the onslaught of
> greed, suspicion, distrust, and cynicism. Visit your
> creation with the spirit of reconciliation, that the
> harmony of love may replace the discord of strife.

For the local community:

> We offer you our community with all its
> strengths and weaknesses, its successes and
> failures. Within the context of our relationships
> there is always a remnant of suffering which
> demands our attention, compassion, and pastoral

response. Make us sensitive to our suffering neighbours in Christ, that we may share their pain and ease their sorrow.

For those in need:

Lord, we are mindful that the sick and the poor, the hungry and the alienated, are a mirror of your Son's suffering and torment. They show us Christ, the suffering servant of mankind. Teach us to perceive the needy not merely as victims of circumstance, but also as ministers of a crucial aspect of your gospel of redemption . . .

For those who have died:

We pray for those who have died; for those who having shared in Christ's ministry of suffering, now reap the reward of his resurrection . . . Each of us has a cross to bear in life. Help us, Lord, that when our time of departure approaches, we may see beyond our cross into the joy of your kingdom.

Finally . . .

Rejoicing in the fellowship of (N and of) all your saints, we commend ourselves and all Christian people to your unfailing love.

The King and the Kingdom: Transfiguration

For the Church:

> Lord, we pray for a Church immersed in the
> politics of temporal life, and too often oblivious
> to the revelation of your Spirit; a Church
> consumed by its continuous struggle to be
> relevant in a complex world, yet often failing to
> heed your voice of counsel. Speak to us, Lord,
> with words we cannot ignore, commands which
> demand our response.

For the world:

> Lord, we lay before you a world soiled by the
> sinfulness of man, nations broken and divided by
> the weight of self-imposed human misery . . .
> Create in us an acute awareness of our folly, and
> a firm resolve to seek you out and rediscover
> your will for us.

For the local community:

> We pray for our community and all of the facets
> of its life . . . Teach us that it is through family
> relationships, human productivity, and intellectual
> curiosity, that you speak to us and make your
> will known. Help us to realize that where there is
> human misunderstanding, your voice of counsel is
> distorted, that when we fail to listen to each
> other, we fail equally to listen to you.

For those in need:

> We offer you the poor and the dispossessed, the hungry and alienated, the lonely and the despairing . . . How often we fail to perceive you in the suffering portion of humanity. In the face of torment you reveal yourself, yet we fail to recognize you. Open our eyes and hearts to detect your presence in every dimension of our lives.

For those who have died:

> We remember those who have died; those to whom, in the act of dying, you have revealed yourself as the great comforter and embodiment of eternal life in the Spirit. By your promise and example, death is no longer final, no longer the end. Rather it marks the beginning of perfect peace and contentment in your presence. Lord, show us the way . . .

Finally . . .

> Rejoicing in the fellowship of (N and of) all your saints, we commend ourselves and all Christian people to your unfailing love.

The King and the Kingdom: Victory of the Cross

For the Church:

> *au ;/ʃ*

> Lord, we pray for the Church, for its ~~clergy and~~
> people . . . Your living community in the world
> shares in the victory of life which you
> accomplished on the cross. Every day, the world
> kills you with its violence and hatred, yet each
> same day, through your Church, you defeat death
> with the power of your love and forgiveness.
> May your people be always blessed with the
> courage and constancy of an abiding faith.

For the world:

> We offer prayers for a world nailed to the cross
> of conflict and war, cruelty and hatred. We mourn
> a world fearful of its own destruction, yet
> demonstrating no active hope of its redemption.
> Lord, speak to your creation of the salvation
> promised to those who trust in a life and peace
> which lies beyond the cross of death and
> suffering.

For the local community:

> Lord, we pray for our local community, for our
> homes and institutions . . . We pray for
> relationships which have deteriorated to the point
> of enmity and dissolution. Remind us that when
> tragedy and sorrow afflict us, Christ's victory of
> peace and love is ours if we but grasp it in faith.

For those in need:

> We pray for those who are in need – those who
> suffer illness, poverty, despair, and estrangement.
> May they see in their own trials a sharing of
> Christ's suffering. May they regard their own
> pain as an expression of Christ's passion, and may
> they look with confident expectations toward
> Christ's redemption.

For those who have died:

> Lord, we remember those who have died and
> discovered the passage to eternal life. Having
> shared in Christ's suffering and death, they now
> also partake of his resurrection . . . May we who
> follow have the courage to share Christ's death
> on the cross as but one step in our own
> pilgrimage to redemption.

Finally . . .

> Rejoicing in the fellowship of (*N* and of) all your
> saints, we commend ourselves and all Christian
> people to your unfailing love.

Way of the Cross

For the Church:

> We pray for the Church as it joins Christ in his
> Palm Sunday progress . . . Too often the Church
> forgets that this procession which begins in
> triumph becomes finally a death march to
> Calvary. Lord, remind Christ's living body that if
> it shares the limelight of Christ's triumph, it must
> also be prepared to share his suffering and death.

For the world:

> Lord, we look in prayer upon a world seemingly
> marching to its own destruction, a civilization
> perversely pursuing its own death . . . It appears
> to be a case of Palm Sunday without Easter. For
> obsessed as they are with temporal power and
> prestige, the world's leaders cannot see beyond
> the cross to the empty tomb; beyond death and
> destruction to a spiritual life of peace. Open their
> eyes, Lord, before it is too late.

For the local community:

> We pray for our community as a spectator of
> Christ's Palm Sunday procession. Like all
> communities, ours has its share of tension,
> divisions, and suffering, which are mirrored in the
> spectacle of our Lord's march to the cross. Help
> us to perceive in the cross of Christ a way to
> renewed life and vitality in our homes and
> institutions.

For those in need:

> Lord, we lay before you the suffering of your
> creation: those who are ill, tormented, and alone
> . . . Remind us that with them Christ has a special
> affinity, that even as he entered Jerusalem in
> triumph, our Lord was himself frightened and
> alone in his ordeal at the hands of his tormentors.

For those who have died:

> Lord, we pray for the souls of those who have
> died – those who have marched to Calvary and
> beyond – those who have journeyed through
> death into the life and peace of your kingdom . . .
> May they rest in peace.

Finally . . .

> Rejoicing in the fellowship of (N and of) all your
> saints, we commend ourselves and all Christian
> people to your unfailing love.

The Lord is Risen

For the Church:

> We offer prayers for the Church and its leaders
> . . . As your living body, the Christian community
> bears active witness to the Easter faith, the good
> news of Christ's resurrection. Help us to realize
> that in a world bristling with the armaments of
> death and destruction, the dissonance of violence
> mocks the harmony of peace, and that in its vigil
> of reconciliation, the Church is lonely and
> vulnerable.

For the world:

> Lord, we pray for a world paralysed by the
> suffering and conflict of the cross, nations lost in
> the darkness of Calvary and blind to the light of
> Easter. Rational man abhors the holocaust of
> death he is capable of unleashing, yet it is man's
> irrational behaviour that often prevails. Protect us,
> Lord, from the insanity of our broken humanity.

For the local community:

> We offer prayers for our community . . . And
> even as we acknowledge the imperfections and
> shortcoming of our communal life, we often
> glimpse signs of resurrection – of new beginnings
> and opportunities – in the reconciliation of
> families and neighbours. Teach us, Lord, that it is

only in the context of this sure hope of wholeness that our struggles and setbacks have any meaning.

For those in need:

Lord, we pray for the suffering of the world, for those whose pilgrimage to resurrection is difficult, painful, and lonely . . . May they find comfort in the knowledge that Jesus charted the same course, that in his own journey to Easter he was himself lonely and despised, rejected and afflicted.

For those who have died:

We offer prayers for those who have emerged from death into eternal life, those in whose resurrection we now rejoice . . . Lord, as we celebrate their Easter faith, may we find in the memory of their spiritual resources a strength for our own witness and a faith in your promise of redemption.

Finally . . .

Rejoicing in the fellowship of (N and of) all your saints, we commend ourselves and all Christian people to your unfailing love.

The Upper Room

For the Church:

Lord, we lay before you a Church newly
reminded of Christ's resurrection – a Church with
new opportunities to be raised with Christ into a
life of witness to the perfection of your love . . .
We pray that the Christian community may
respond to its deliverance in the spirit of renewed
faith and commitment, that in a world dark with
despair and pain, the light of your redemption
may prevail.

For the world:

We pray for a world teeming with violence and
hostility, a world that crucifies you again and
again with its hatred and conflict . . . Now in the
Easter season you offer your rebellious children
yet another opportunity to live in mutual peace
and interdependence. You offer love in response
to hatred, trust in response to suspicion, and
reconciliation in response to the tensions of
violence and conflict. May those in authority
accept your offering and be raised with you to a
new awareness of your redeeming will.

For the local community:

We offer up to you our local community – our
schools, businesses and homes . . . We pray that
the light of Easter may illumine the shadows of
our relationships, that the love which conquers

death may bind us together in the spirit of mutual faith and respect, and that we may respond to your risen presence with unreserved trust and a commitment to placing your love at the very centre of our communal life.

For those in need:

We pray for those in need, for the sick and the poor . . . We pray especially for those who are frightened, cynical, and without the faith to sustain them. Visit them in their doubts and scepticism, that they may at last know that you are the love, peace, and comfort in whom they may find health and strength.

For those who have died:

Lord, we remember those who have died, those whose faith has sustained them and carried them through into your kingdom . . . As witnesses to their commitment and trust in your love, may we discover for ourselves the faith which keeps us alive and attuned to the power of your risen Son.

Finally . . .

Rejoicing in the fellowship of (N and of) all your saints, we commend ourselves and all Christian people to your unfailing love.

The Bread of Life

For the Church:

Lord, we pray for the Church, that community of witness through which you nourish and sustain the world . . . All too often, the Church becomes bogged down and immobilized by the rigidity of its laws and doctrines, its codes of practice and precedence. Remind the Church, Lord, that its true life is not in law, but in Christ's Spirit, that its true power derives not from doctrine, but rather from the spirit of love, compassion, and forgiveness which Christ embodies.

For the world:

We lay before you a world lost in the wilderness of its own folly, a world hungry for your love, yet consumed by its own hatred and ambition. We pray for nations and governments desperate for life and peace, yet engaged in the trading of death and conflict . . . Lord, release us from the prison of our perversity and blindness, that we may be nourished by your spirit of reconciliation and thereby seize the victory of life which you offer.

For the local community:

We pray for the life of our community, for the relationships between its people . . . We are reminded that prosperity is not merely a matter of well manicured gardens and well stocked refrigerators. Rather the true wealth of a community is measured in terms of the depth of its spiritual and moral foundations, the strength of its commitment to your principles of love, charity and compassion.

For those in need:

We offer you the suffering portion of your creation, those who are in physical and spiritual need, whose quality of life has been blighted by accident or disease . . . They seek the nourishment of your spirit to comfort them in their distress, to alleviate their pain. Visit them in the darkness of their fears and anxieties with the reassurance that your own portion of suffering was but a prelude to the banquet of eternal life.

For those who have died:

We celebrate the memory of those who have died, those who partake of the bread of eternal life at the great banquet of resurrection. Freed from the shackles of sin and human folly, they now live in the freedom of your perfect love. Turn our eyes outward from our self concerns, that we may have a clearer perception of the true life which you promise to all of your children.

Finally . . .

Rejoicing in the fellowship of *(N* and *of)* all your saints, we commend ourselves and all Christian people to your unfailing love.

The Emmaus Road

For the Church:

> We lay before you your Church, the living body
> of Christ who is a stranger to so many of your
> children . . . In a world hungry for peace, may the
> Church's eucharistic banquet be a source of
> nourishment in which nations recognize the
> loving presence of Christ in their midst.

For the world:

> We pray for the world, its nations and
> governments. We behold a world in which
> millions of God's children starve in the midst of
> plenty. Remind us, Lord, that just as you fed
> thousands with a few loaves and fishes, so it is
> the moral obligation of a world rich in
> agricultural resources to distribute them in such a
> way that hunger no longer ravages its people . . .

For the local community:

> We offer prayers for our local community and its
> families, the affluent and the poor. Every day you
> join us on the road of our daily lives. You sit at
> the table with us, revealing yourself as the source
> of our many blessings. Teach us to share these
> blessings with others who are less fortunate than
> ourselves, that we may be nourished by your
> abiding presence and recognize you as the Lord
> of our life.

For those in need:

We pray for those in need, those who are in physical pain or mental darkness, whose banquet of life has been sparse and bitter . . . You sit with them at table, Lord, revealing yourself as the source of comfort and health. Open the hearts and minds of the suffering to recognize you as the power to transform bitterness into forbearance, resignation into trust and hope.

For those who have died:

We pray for those who have died, and now see you totally revealed at the feast of resurrection . . . On the road of earthly life you are too often a stranger, unrecognized – disguised by our temporal concerns and passions. May we, like those who have gone before us, finally see you not darkly, but face to face. May we enter your kingdom and discover for ourselves the ultimate blessing of your clear and present love.

Finally . . .

Rejoicing in the fellowship of (N and of) all your saints, we commend ourselves and all Christian people to your unfailing love.

The Good Shepherd

For the Church:

> We lay before you your Church, the appointed shepherd of your earthly flock. As members of your living body, we confess that we are not always diligent, that external pressures and influences often divert us from the true nature of our task, that the compulsion to be popular in the midst of predators often exposes your sheep to mortal danger. Strengthen us with renewed commitment and resolve, that our pastoral witness may be secure.

For the world:

> We pray for a world whose pastures are teeming with wolves of greed and exploitation, nations in which the continuing struggle for power and political ascendancy often is carried out at the expense of human decency and compassion. We pray for governments who impose their authority in such a way that the rights of their citizens are ignored . . . Turn the hearts of the world's leaders that their commitment to leadership may be sacrificial rather than exploitative, that they may serve rather than manipulate.

For the local community:

> We offer you our (village, town, etc.), praying especially for officials of our local government . . . Having been elected to serve their constituents,

may they shape policies which work to the benefit and prosperity of all sections of the community. And may they have the vision to look beyond local boundaries into the community at large.

For those in need:

We pray for those who are in need – for the sick, the poor, and those who are vulnerable to manipulation and exploitation. We pray especially for the ministries of priests, doctors, and other personnel who care for them, that the practical help which they offer may always be motivated by your love, always mixed with a generous portion of genuine and deeply felt pastoral concern . . .

For those who have died:

We remember those who have died, those whom the good shepherd has taken into his spiritual fold . . . Having responded to his voice of promise and redemption, they have followed him home to his kingdom of peace and light. Eternal rest grant unto them, O Lord, etc.

Finally . . .

Rejoicing in the fellowship of (N and of) all your saints, we commend ourselves and all Christian people to your unfailing love.

The Lakeside

For the Church:

Lord, we pray for the Church, your living body of discipleship whose net of witness and evangelism is wide but vulnerable. As fishers of men, we reap a meagre harvest because our identity is often confused. All too often we accommodate ourselves to the object of our evangelism, thereby ignoring the Lord whom we are called to serve. Recall your Church, Lord, to the true nature of its calling, that she may again be a persuasive and attractive force in the midst of indifference and hostility . . .

For the world:

We pray for a fragmented world. For nations and governments in conflict . . . We pray especially for the world's leaders, for those whose power and authority are the implements of a secular and political ministry on behalf of their people. It is with great sadness and anger that we observe the perversion of this ministry, the wielding of temporal authority not in compassion or for the good of mankind, but rather with brutality to oppress and destroy the human spirit. In too many corridors of power, despotism overwhelms statesmanship, and a world created strong and vital is divided and grievously wounded. Save us, Lord, from our folly.

For the local community:

We lay before you our community, our families and institutions. We offer prayers for our schools whose ministry of education and enlightenment is critical in the wisdom and effectiveness of our communal life ... Bless our teachers with the vision, skill, and patience to fire the imagination and curiosity of their pupils, that they may bring to the problems of a complex world the spirit of intellectual and spiritual confidence and maturity.

For those in need:

We pray for those in need, the community of suffering whose ministry to the healthy is one of stoicism and courage ... By their bravery in the face of adversity, they make us humble in our comfort. And we pray that being mindful of our own good fortune, we may respond to suffering with a ministry of comfort and compassion.

For those who have died:

We remember the departed, those who have died in the Lord, and are now alive with him in the midst of his perfect love. Being raised with Christ, they provide us with grounds for hope in our own redemption. May we discover in their example this ministry of the great possibilities open to us in the life and resurrection of our Lord ...

Finally ...

Rejoicing in the fellowship of (N and of) all your saints, we commend ourselves and all Christian people to your unfailing love.

The Resurrection and the Life

For the Church:

> We pray for the Church, that vast community of
> faith appointed to embody the hope of
> resurrection . . . May your disciples never lose
> their optimism and conviction that in spite of the
> surrounding darkness of human cruelty and
> despair, the light of your love and salvation is
> eternal and inextinguishable.

For the world:

> We pray for a world that has lost its way,
> nations whose spiritual focus has become blurred
> and distorted, leaders whose faith in the strength
> of compassion has been perverted into self-
> adulation and a lust for personal power . . . There
> is in the human spirit a great capacity to rise
> above its baser instincts. Deep in the human soul
> you have planted the seeds of love and
> understanding. Bring them to fruition, Lord, that
> the world may be healed.

For the local community:

> We lay before you our local community — its
> homes and institutions, its people and their
> talents. We are especially mindful of those whose
> abiding commitment is to the development of
> local and indigenous resources, those whose firm
> faith in the richness and potential of our
> community has given it vitality and strength . . .

For those in need:

> We pray for our brothers and sisters in
> adversity – those who are sick, poor, frightened,
> alone . . . For them, life has been reduced to mere
> existence; faith in your power and will to heal is
> difficult for them to sustain. Visit them in all their
> pain and vulnerability with the assurance that in
> your love there is comfort and the promise of
> renewal.

For those who have died:

> We remember those who have died, those whose
> faith in resurrection has been rewarded . . . As
> they look upon us from the incomparable peace
> of your kingdom, they observe in sorrow the
> turmoil of our lives, the fitfulness of our faith.
> Renew us, Lord, that our witness to your spiritual
> gifts may lift us above the world's conflicts and
> into the serenity of your eternal presence.

Finally . . .

> Rejoicing in the fellowship of (*N* and of) all your
> saints, we commend ourselves and all Christian
> people to your unfailing love.

The Charge to Peter

For the Church:

> Lord, we lay before you your Church, that
> community of faith appointed to be the faithful
> guardians of a troubled world, called by you to
> work in the world until you return . . . We
> confess a weak and fitful discipleship, a witness
> which is often weak and irresolute. Give us the
> strength and the courage to meet the world's
> indifference and hostility with your spiritual
> power of love and reconciliation.

For the world:

> We offer you the world, a global city in
> desperate need of your restoration and the
> guidance of your ruling presence. Corruption,
> hatred, and greed have raised up conflict in our
> midst. Violence has become our only answer to
> dispute and controversy . . . Yet by your
> resurrection you demonstrate the futility and
> impotence of cruelty. Forgiveness is your answer
> to brutality. Raise us, Lord, to a greater and more
> comprehensive awareness of your will.

For the local community:

> We pray for our community – our families,
> schools, and businesses – and for those
> individuals with whom we have daily contact and
> relationships . . . It is in this more personal and
> intimate context of our lives that your charge of

discipleship is of critical importance. It is at the local community level that our witness to your love, our demonstration of compassion, has a direct and positive effect on human relationships. Revive our devotion to you, Lord; renew us in our witness, that we may be ever more aware of our importance in your will to redeem.

For those in need:

Lord, we offer you those in need, those whose call to discipleship is a very special one, whose witness reaches a very deep and vital portion of our soul . . . It is our suffering brothers and sisters who remind us most poignantly of our many blessings. It is they who make us most clearly aware of your grace. Such reminders are often painful, Lord, yet without them we are not spiritually complete. Have mercy, Lord.

For those who have died:

We remember those who have died, those who, having demonstrated a commitment to Christ which sustained them in the world, now find their reward in the peace and light of your kingdom . . . We give thanks for their discipleship, for the compassion and love they have shown to friends and relations. And we pray that we may find in their example the power to renew our own faith in your promises.

Finally . . .

Rejoicing in the fellowship of (N and of) all your saints, we commend ourselves and all Christian people to your unfailing love.

73

The Way, the Truth, and the Life

For the Church:

> We pray for the Church as it struggles to
> embody Christ's living body in the midst of the
> death of human conflict and hatred. Never has the
> way of peace and love been more elusive and
> more difficult to follow. Lord, raise up leaders of
> vision and sacrificial dedication, that the way of
> Christ may indeed be alive and well in the world.

For the world:

> We offer up the nations and the leaders of the
> world for your blessing and renewal. We pray for
> governments and citizens of the weak and poor
> nations as they struggle to find their identity, to
> discover the truth of their importance and rights
> in global affairs. Remind us, Lord, that until the
> small and vulnerable communities of the world
> are shown the way to prosperity and self respect,
> there can be no peace, no reconciliation, in the
> community of nations as a whole.

For the local community:

> We pray for our local community and its leaders
> . . . May our elected officials promote the spirit of
> co-operation and integrity which binds us
> together in a continuing process of renewal and
> self belief. Instil in us the conviction that we have
> the capacity to shape our community into a
> proper earthly reflection of Christ's kingdom.

For those in need:

> Lord, we lay before you those who are in need,
> those whose way in the world is hard, whose
> faith in God's goodness does not come easily . . .
> In those who are bitter and cynical, plant the
> spirit of patience and forbearance, that they may
> see in you the Lord of healing and spiritual
> renewal.

For those who have died:

> Lord, we remember those who have died, those
> whose faith and witness are a continuing
> inspiration to us . . . Having discovered the way
> into your eternal presence, the truth of your
> resurrection promise, may we discover our own
> key to a life of the spirit; may we follow them to
> our own portion of your eternal glory.

Finally . . .

> Rejoicing in the fellowship of (N and of) all your
> saints, we commend ourselves and all Christian
> people to your unfailing love.

Going to the Father

For the Church:

> Lord, we raise up to you your Church, that body
> of faith through whom you would save the world
> . . . In its ministry of reconciliation, the Church
> encounters much that is seemingly irreconcilable.
> In its witness to your inexhaustable love and
> forgiveness, the Church finds much that provokes
> anger and is unforgivable. Fill your disciples with
> the patience and forbearance to be Christ in all
> things and to all people.

For the world:

> We pray for a world adrift in the chaos of its
> own making, for nations who provoke your
> anger, for leaders who mock you and have lost
> sight of their true allegiance in a self-serving lust
> for power and influence . . . Lord, raise up leaders
> of statesmanship, self-effacing governments who
> seek the welfare of their people, that we may be
> reminded of the love and compassion that is at
> the heart of your judgement.

For the local community:

> We offer you our community, the families and
> individuals among whom our personal influence
> and aspirations are most directly felt. In this
> context we have a rare opportunity to
> demonstrate your saving power by our own

individual witness, to be Christlike in our relationships, to denounce cruelty and injustice, and to promote the spirit of reconciliation.

For those in need:

Lord, we pray for those in need, for those who are perhaps the closest to the true focus of Christ's ministry . . . Teach us, Lord, that by caring for the sick and the poor, by demonstrating concern and compassion for the lonely and the hungry, we are at the same time showing our love for, our allegiance to, the Christ whom we serve.

For those who have died:

We remember those who have died, those who have gone to the Father and are at rest in his kingdom . . . For them the saving power of Christ has been proved, the risen Christ has drawn them up into his embrace of love. May there be a place for us beside them.

Finally . . .

Rejoicing in the fellowship of (N and of) all your saints, we commend ourselves and all Christian people to your unfailing love.

The Ascension of Christ

For the Church:

> Lord, we offer up to you your Church, that
> minority of disciples whom you left in the world
> at your ascension to be your living presence and
> witness until your return . . . May the Church
> bear ever stronger and more persuasive testimony
> to your capacity for love and reconciliation, your
> will to direct the lives of your rebellious children.
> May the life of the Church always be a
> persuasive example of that which your creation
> has the capacity to become.

For the world:

> We pray for a world floundering on the shoals of
> self-delusion, imprisoned in the tragedy of war
> and cynicism. You are present in the midst of
> nations, yet your authority is largely ignored.
> You speak in the prophecy of statesmen and
> visionaries, yet their message is mocked and your
> voice falls on the deaf ears of selfishness and
> greed. Do not forsake us, Lord; speak to us until
> we must finally listen.

For the local community:

> We pray for our local community, especially for
> those who exert a pastoral influence upon our
> families and homes. Bestow upon our doctors and
> nurses a generous portion of your healing

power — fill ministers and councillors with your
capacity to create peace and harmony in human
lives — that until you return again to reconcile us
with your perfect will, we may enjoy a foretaste
of that kingdom which is to come.

For those in need:

We offer you the suffering portion of your
creation, those who are a special concern of your
compassion and love, those whom you bore
especially in mind when you left the world in the
care of your disciples. May the needy of this
world always inspire in us an acute sense of
humility and thanksgiving for the many blessings
you have given us . . .

For those who have died:

We pray for those who have died, those who
have ascended with Christ to live with him in
your kingdom . . . As we celebrate the ultimate
fulfilment of their resurrection faith, may our own
witness be strengthened as we strive to embody
the risen and ascended Christ in our daily lives.

Finally . . .

Rejoicing in the fellowship of (*N* and of) all your
saints, we commend ourselves and all Christian
people to your unfailing love.

The Spirit of God is Given to Man

For the Church:

> We offer prayers for your Church set in the
> context of a multicultural, multiracial, society, a
> Church called upon to preach a gospel which
> transcends the boundaries of colour and creed.
> We pray that the Church may take the initiative
> in promoting the equality of all mankind, that the
> scope of your love, the gift of your Holy Spirit,
> may be truly universal and unrestricted.

For the world:

> We pray for a world in which the cancer of
> racism is far advanced, often underscored by
> religious bigotry and intolerance. This morning
> we ask your forgiveness for having wandered
> from the true spirit of Pentecost, for having
> forgotten and ignored the message of those
> tongues of flame which are truly universal, that
> spirit of salvation which is offered to all nations,
> and which should bind the world together in
> peace and harmony. Lord, raise again this spirit in
> the world's consciousness, that mankind may be
> turned back from the brink of its own demise.

For the local community:

> We offer prayers for our local community,
> especially for the minority groups who live and
> work in our midst . . . Make us mindful, Lord, of
> their insecurity and fear, give them courage in the
> process of racial and cultural integration, and raise

up in our parish the spirit of true acceptance and hospitality, that indeed all of our neighbours may be filled with an awareness of Christ's universal love and reconciliation.

For those in need:

We pray for those who are in need, particularly those who are unloved and ostracized because of racial and cultural prejudice, those who do not receive their fair share of society's care and compassion because they are different from the majority, those who with Christ are 'despised and rejected of men' . . . Teach us, Lord, that prejudice is the ultimate perversion of Christ's gospel, that to turn one's back on even the smallest portion of God's children is to turn one's back on Christ himself and spurn the universal love and redemption which he offers. Turn our hearts, Lord, that we may bring you back into our lives.

For those who have died:

We remember the departed, those who have discovered in God's kingdom the full realization of his love, the all embracing scope of his salvation . . . Just as in Christ there is no discrimination, so too may we be indiscriminate in our demonstration of his love and concern, thereby preparing ourselves for glory with him in eternity.

Finally . . .

Rejoicing in the fellowship of (N and of) all your saints, we commend ourselves and all Christian people to your unfailing love.

The Threefold Nature of God

For the Church:

> Lord, we pray for your Church and its leaders . . .
> Too often the Church becomes obsessed with
> doctrine, enmeshed in legalistic detail to the
> detriment of its faith, its spontaneous response to
> the breath of your Spirit, the demands of your
> will. Visit your Church in all the dimensions of
> your being, set her free to trust and respond to
> your spiritual gifts.

For the world:

> We lay before you a world created to be saved,
> yet by its own folly seemingly doomed to
> destruction. We pray for nations built upon the
> foundations of law and order, yet who pervert
> this law to sow the seeds of violence, cruelty, and
> global disorder . . . Lord, raise up leaders who
> have the vision to perceive law not as the master
> of policy, but rather the servant of instinct and
> ordinances which are humane and compassionate,
> responsive to your spirit of love and redemption.

For the local community:

> We pray for our (village, town, etc.) and its
> people. Remind us, Lord that the strength of our
> community lies in its diversity. Break down the
> barriers of discrimination and class distinction
> which divide us and weaken the fabric of our

corporate life. Teach us that just as there are three aspects of your person and power, so are there many dimensions of experience which contribute to the depth and richness of our communal relationships.

For those in need:

We pray for those in need, those whose pain, loneliness, and anxieties prevent them from responding positively to your healing presence in their lives . . . In their distress and vulnerability they grasp at straws, seizing upon virtually anything that promises relief from their suffering. Visit them in the assurance that you are the one and supreme healer, the true source of comfort, hope and peace.

For those who have died:

We remember those who have died, those who now see and experience the fulness of your nature and power . . . For them the Trinity and other doctrines, which are a mystery to us, appear of no consequence in the clear light of your eternal presence. You are with them in your kingdom — this is the simple truth of resurrection. Be with us, however darkly, that we may have a glimpse of that which is to come.

Finally . . .

Rejoicing in the fellowship of (N and of) all your saints, we commend ourselves and all Christian people to your unfailing love.

SECOND SUNDAY
AFTER PENTECOST

(Trinity 1)

The People of God

For the Church:

> Lord, we bring before you your Church, the
> living body of your son through whom the new
> covenant of redemption is made with mankind.
> We pray especially for the ordained ministry,
> commissioned to be spokesmen for Christ in the
> world . . . Renew them with an acute awareness
> of their responsibility to promote and exemplify
> spiritual honesty and integrity in the midst of
> their people.

For the world:

> We pray for a world bristling with destructive
> power, nations who pervert your covenant of
> love and reconciliation into contracts which
> provide for the distribution of arms and other
> vehicles of death and destruction. The hand of
> friendship has become the fist of violence, and we
> watch in dismay as the peace you leave with us
> is shattered again and again by the cacophony of
> war . . .

For the local community:

> Lord, we offer you our community, a people
> chosen to live together in the spirit of peace and
> mutual concern, to relate to one another in the
> spirit of reconciliation and mutual respect. Yet

how often the discord of aggression and
selfishness mars the harmony we would establish.
Bind us together, Lord, and by the cords of your
spirit make us your people.

For those in need:

We pray for that portion of your people who are
in need, whose faith in your covenant of
compassion is strained by the pain and anxiety
which afflicts them . . . Remind those who suffer
that the suffering Christ is very close to them,
that his victory over pain is theirs as well.

For those who have died:

Lord, we pray for those who have died, those
whose contract of redemption has been honoured
in being raised with Christ into his kingdom . . .
In our own privileged position as Christ's
disciples, help us to honour our covenant of faith
and witness, that we too may ultimately rest in
the eternal peace of your salvation.

Finally . . .

Rejoicing in the fellowship of (N and of) all your
saints, we commend ourselves and all Christian
people to your unfailing love.

The Church's Unity and Fellowship

For the Church:

> We pray for your Church and its leaders . . . As
> your spiritual community in the world, may your
> disciples demonstrate the fellowship and cohesion
> necessary to serve as an example of the love and
> interdependence which should bind all your
> children together.

For the world:

> We offer you a world in disarray, nations living
> in increasing isolation from one another, and who
> are so protective of their own interests that the
> prosperity and welfare of others are at grave risk
> . . . Teach them, Lord, that the health and vitality
> of society at large depends upon a strong bond
> of fellowship and mutual concern, a profound
> commitment to share one another's burdens.

For the local community:

> We lay before you our community and the
> relationships upon which it is based. We pray
> especially for those community projects which
> promote new relationships and fellowship in our
> midst, those which strengthen the bonds of
> mutual sensitivity and concern which enrich our
> corporate life . . . 'Keep us ever mindful, Lord, of
> each other's needs.'

For those in need:

We pray for those in need – the sick, the poor, and especially those whom it is difficult to love, those whom we instinctively ostracize because it requires too much effort to include them in our fellowship. We pray for them in their isolation and loneliness, and we ask forgiveness for our own selfishness.

For those who have died:

We remember those who have died, those who have joined that perfect community of God's saints in his kingdom ... We pray that our own attempts to establish a fellowship of compassion and reconciliation here on earth may prepare us for that perfect unity which will be ours in heaven.

Finally ...

Rejoicing in the fellowship of (*N* and of) all your saints, we commend ourselves and all Christian people to your unfailing love.

THIRD SUNDAY
AFTER PENTECOST
(Trinity 2)

The Life of the Baptized

For the Church:

> We offer prayers for the Church, its clergy and
> people . . . As members of Christ's earthly
> community, remind us that at the heart of our
> ministry is the force of Baptism — rebirth in the
> spirit of love. Whether it be in the sacrament
> itself, or in our daily witness to the regeneration
> of our own lives, we pray for constancy in the
> obedience of your one great commandment to
> love and forgive one another.

For the world:

> We pray for a world in travail, a world in pain,
> cut off from your renewing love by its obstinacy
> and folly . . . Above the heads of your children
> the waters of Baptism, the streams of living
> water, are poised to flow, but are repudiated by
> human arrogance and conceit. And so mankind
> drives itself toward a dismal end, ignoring its
> creator's will to cleanse, regenerate, and redeem.
> Make us aware of our peril, Lord, that in the
> spirit of contrition we may be saved.

For the local community:

> We pray for our community and its life, for our
> homes and schools . . . We are reminded that it is
> primarily through the local community that we as

individuals can exert an influence upon the quality of life to which we aspire. It is in the community structure that our witness to the principles of Christ can be most keenly felt. Help us, Lord, that by our example, the power of our Lord may be born anew in the spirit of fairness and compassion for all its citizens.

For those in need:

We offer prayers for those in need, the sick, the poor, and especially those without a faith to sustain them . . . Teach us, Lord, that those who suffer require an extra portion of our concern and compassion, a concentrated participation in that new life of spiritual power into which we are all baptized. Lord, make us generous in sharing those spiritual gifts which you offer us.

For those who have died:

We remember those who have departed this life, and are now baptized in the glory of resurrection . . . Having shared with Christ the death of the body, they are now raised with him into the life of the spirit. Make us worthy, that when the time comes for us to leave this world, we too may find our way into the eternal light of paradise.

Finally . . .

Rejoicing in the fellowship of (N and of) all your saints, we commend ourselves and all Christian people to your unfailing love.

The Church's Confidence in Christ

For the Church:

> Lord, we offer prayers for your Church in the
> world. And for its leaders who place their
> confidence in the spirit of Christ's love and his
> promise of salvation . . . All too often, the Church
> becomes smug and self-satisfied in its ministry,
> basking in its ecclesiastical ingenuity, and
> forgetting that whatever talents it demonstrates
> come from you. In these times of spiritual
> arrogance, visit your Church in the spirit of
> humility, that it may identify you as the true and
> only source of its evangelism.

For the world:

> We pray for a world ignorant of its creator,
> nations and leaders lost in the darkness of self-
> seeking arrogance and pride . . . As governments
> pursue their own ends, mindful only of their
> selfish passions and ambition, remind them that
> they are but stewards of your creation, that
> without your will to create and sustain, human
> society and its aspirations have no substance or
> meaning.

For the local community:

> We pray for our community, especially those
> whose vocation it is to remind us of the

principles of love and compassion which bind us together and make us strong . . . Remind us also, Lord, that many of your most devoted disciples do not wear collars or boast titles and degrees. Rather, they work anonymously and tirelessly in the community and family to promote that spirit of human dignity and pride which ennobles us all.

For those in need:

We pray for those who are vulnerable to exploitation, those whose confidence in the healing power of Christ has been severely shaken by misfortune, fear, and anxiety . . . May they perceive something of Christ's healing presence in our ministry of compassion, the love and concern, the care, that we offer them.

For those who have died:

We celebrate the memory of those who have died, those whose confidence in Christ and his promise of resurrection has been amply rewarded . . . May their steadfastness, the constancy of their faith be an inspiration to us whose witness is often faltering and insecure. May we discover the deep resources of commitment that will ultimately carry us forward into the peace and joy of God's kingdom.

Finally . . .

Rejoicing in the fellowship of (N and of) all your saints, we commend ourselves and all Christian people to your unfailing love.

The Freedom of the Sons of God

For the Church:

> We pray for your Church and its leaders . . . How
> weak, divided, and immature your living body in
> the world appears; how singularly unprepared for
> the great ministry to which it is called. Surely the
> time has come for your disciples to come of age,
> yet how far they seem from the mark. Your
> gospel is a message for mature minds and faithful
> hearts. Bring your Church to fruition that it may
> do your will in a troubled and complex world.

For the world:

> We offer you, Lord, a world at the crossroads,
> nations faced with hard decisions effecting their
> very survival . . . We pray for leaders of nations,
> men of power, who are enslaved by their own
> greed, fear, insecurity, and suspicions. Time is
> short and we pray for deliverance, that the
> appointed time of your redemption may soon be
> upon us.

For the local community:

> We pray for our local community, especially
> those families and individuals who are in conflict,
> and among whom the seeds of dissent and
> distrust have been sown. Such discord weakens
> the whole fabric of community relations, and we

pray for a time when trust and harmony may create peace, strength, and stability in our communal life.

For those in need:

We pray for the suffering portion of your creation, those who are overwhelmed by pain, imprisoned by anxiety, loneliness, and rejection ... Lord, set them free – release them from the bonds of bitterness and cynicism, that they may look with hope and trust to a more healthy and productive life.

For those who have died:

We remember the departed, those who have finally come of age, and have been chosen by God to share the glory of his kingdom ... May we, by the constancy of our faith, by our steadfast obedience of Christ's new commandment of mutual love, be adopted as partakers of the risen life which he promises.

Finally ...

Rejoicing in the fellowship of (N and of) all your saints, we commend ourselves and all Christian people to your unfailing love.

The Church's Mission to the Individual

For the Church:

> Lord, we pray for the Church and its ministry,
> being especially mindful of those whose ideas and
> convictions determine the focus of the Church's
> evangelism . . . Teach us, Lord, that although the
> Church is a corporate body, a community of
> witness, yet it is also the body of Christ, an
> individual whose spiritual perfection and ministry
> of love is the source of its life.

For the world:

> We lay before you a world in which the clash of
> personalities, the battle between individual wills
> and egos has produced a state of grave danger
> and instability. In many nations, power and
> authority are exercised to crush aspirations and
> break the human spirit . . . Bring human society
> into harmony with your will, that peace and
> prosperity may at last heal your broken and
> divided world.

For the local community:

> We pray for our local community and its life. We
> ask that you raise up men and women who will
> have the will and capacity to assume positions of
> authority and influence. As individual members of
> the community, we examine ourselves and the

contribution that we do, or do not, make to the corporate welfare. It is too easy to blame others for our own shortcomings, and we pray for the humility to make an honest assessment of our performance and to respond accordingly.

For those in need:

We pray for those who are in need of your special love, individuals who are cut off from society and community life by virtue of illness or prejudice . . . We pray especially for those whose eccentricity and non-conformity make them unacceptable to the majority, outcasts in the eyes of society at large. Remind us, Lord, that it is for the suffering minority that Christ shows his greatest compassion; to them he reaches out his arms of love and acceptance.

For those who have died:

We remember loved ones who have died – those whose memory is dear to us, whose example of faith we take as our own inspiration . . . For each of them God has a special care, a special love; to each of them he offers the gift of his risen life. May we never lose our confidence in Christ and his will to save us who endure to the end.

Finally . . .

Rejoicing in the fellowship of (N and of) all your saints, we commend ourselves and all Christian people to your unfailing love.

FIFTH SUNDAY
AFTER PENTECOST
(Trinity 4)

The New Law

For the Church:

> Lord, we pray for your Church and its leaders . . .
> As a community called to sustain your new law
> of love and reconciliation, we pray in sadness for
> those authorities who are still enslaved by the old
> and rigid law of dogma and legalism. Free them
> from these constraints, that the whole Church
> may be ruled by your spirit of charity and
> compassion.

For the world:

> We pray for a world in which the rule of law is
> constantly flouted in the quest for power and
> authority, nations and governments in which laws
> seem made to be broken in the wake of ambition
> and greed. Remind us, Lord, that in the scheme of
> human affairs, society must be subject to a code
> of conduct, an order imposed by law, if it is to be
> stable and productive; at the same time, we pray
> that such laws as are necessary be motivated
> always by the spirit of Christ's command that we
> love and care for one another.

For the local community:

> We pray for our community and its institutions,
> especially for those who are engaged in the
> interpretation and enforcement of laws which

regulate our community life . . . May the law
enforcement always be tempered by your spirit of
compassion, that we may be liberated to respond
responsibly and charitably to the needs of our
community.

For those in need:

We offer you the poor and the oppressed, those
in need of Christ's special love and compassion
. . . It is with their needs and vulnerability in
mind that the laws of society must be
constructed, regulations which enable those who
suffer to share to the fullest possible extent the
richness and variety of community life.

For those who have died:

We remember those who have died, those who
are fully liberated by the perfect love and peace
of your kingdom . . . May we who follow them,
whose liberation is incomplete, discover in our
striving to obey Christ's law of love a foretaste
of the perfection that is to come.

Finally . . .

Rejoicing in the fellowship of (N and of) all the
saints, we commend ourselves and all Christian
people to your unfailing love.

The Church's Mission to All Men

For the Church:

> We pray for the Church throughout the world,
> for the body of Christ which permits no racial,
> cultural, or denominational divisions or prejudices
> . . . Because the leadership of the Church is
> subject to human failings, we know that the
> universal ideal is not always realized. Black and
> white parishes rarely mix; denominations of
> Christendom stand aloof from each other. Bring
> us together, Lord, that the broken body of your
> son may be healed.

For the world:

> We lay before you a broken world, a world blind
> to its inherent unity, nations in constant
> competition for power and individual supremacy
> . . . Remind us, Lord, that the ultimate authority
> and power are yours, that the scope of your
> kingdom covers all mankind. Turn our attention
> outward from our own selfish concerns, that we
> may perceive the common desires and needs
> which bind the global family together.

For the local community:

> We pray for our community and the life that we
> all share in common. How easy it is to be self-
> centred in our concerns, to forget that one

person's success or tragedy has universal implications. How many neighbourhoods there are where the family next door is an unknown quantity. In short, Lord, remind us that we *are* a community, that we are, in a profound sense, our brother's keeper.

For those in need:

We offer you those in need, those who suffer and are lonely . . . Let us not forget that they have a special place in your concern, that Christ's message of hope and new beginnings is intended for them in a very special way, enabling them to see beyond their suffering to the process of healing.

For those who have died:

We remember those who have departed this life. And we give thanks that at the resurrection, all races, all cultures, all Christian denominations are equal in your sight, with equal access to your kingdom . . . Teach us, Lord, that in the risen life, all of the prejudices which we nurture in the world are broken down and become irrelevant in the context of your eternal and universal love.

Finally . . .

Rejoicing in the fellowship of (N and of) all your saints, we commend ourselves and all Christian people to your unfailing love.

The New Man

For the Church:

> Lord, we lay before you your Church, the body
> of your Son in which the new relationship
> between you and your creation is personified. We
> pray especially for the clergy and other ministers,
> that in their lives and witness, the indwelling
> presence of Christ and his love may be seen at
> work ... Make forgiveness the cornerstone of
> their ministry, that even the most rebellious of
> your children may have access to the new life
> which you offer.

For the world:

> We pray for a rebellious, often hateful, world, for
> nations and leaders who commit acts of
> unforgivable barbarism against their fellow
> creatures, by whom crimes against humanity are
> perpetrated in the name of firm authority and
> government ... Even as we realize the depth of
> our sin, we know that even the slightest gesture
> of contrition would elicit your forgiveness and
> offer of reconciliation. Turn your creation, Lord,
> in the very depths of its perversity, that it may
> come to you as the only source of its renewal.

For the local community:

> We offer you our community and the
> relationships which bind it together. We pray

especially for the intimate relations within families
and between friends, relationships rooted in the
new law of love and trust which Christ
personifies, relationships which show Christ, alive
and well, to the world. Yet our family life does
not always live up to your expectations, Lord,
and we pray for the perception to see you as the
strengthener of bonds that enliven us.

For those in need:

We pray for those who are in need, who are
vulnerable to pain and anxiety, who await your
renewing power . . . For them it is difficult to
believe, to have faith in a new life of peace, a
new beginning in the spirit of hope. Yet it is this
that you offer, and we pray that their hearts may
be opened to receive you and be healed.

For those who have died:

We commemorate those who have died, those
who have been made new in the peace of your
kingdom . . . They have lived the life of a
prodigal in the world, yet you reclaim them in
the spirit of love and forgiveness; you offer them
a new life in your presence. 'Forgive us our
trespasses,' Lord, that we may ultimately be
reunited with our loved ones in your kingdom.

Finally . . .

Rejoicing in the fellowship of (N and of) all your
saints, we commend ourselves and all Christian
people to your unfailing love.

SEVENTH SUNDAY
AFTER PENTECOST
(Trinity 6)

The More Excellent Way

For the Church:

> We pray for the Church as it strives to follow the
> way of Christ, for the Church's leaders in their
> calling to treat human frailty in the spirit of
> patience and forgiveness. Yet how much cruelty
> and suffering are caused in the name of religion
> and the Church: how the Church has offended
> you under cover of zeal and passion. How little
> forgiveness there is in the letter of the law. Teach
> your Church the art of compassion, Lord, that the
> letter of the law may be overruled by its spirit.

For the world:

> We pray for a world that has lost its way, for
> governments and leaders who reject your love for
> the love of self . . . Like Israel, we are a rebellious
> people. And even as you punished your chosen
> people, so do you vent your anger upon us by
> the tragic peril in which we now find ourselves.
> Our only hope, our only comfort, is to be found
> in our faith that your love overcomes your
> vengeance, that your compassion is stronger than
> your anger. Stay with us, Lord, that we may be
> saved.

For the local community:

> We offer you our community, our families and
> relationships in which the spirit of your love

should be dominant. We pray in sorrow for relations which are loveless and based upon convention and propriety, relationships which have virtually died, but which are resuscitated and perpetuated for the sake of appearance and self-delusion. If it be your will, Lord, make us more mature in the formation of relationships, breathe new life into our marital and social commitments, that your way of love and reconciliation may be our way of renewing the strength and vitality of our community life.

For those who are in need:

Lord, we pray for those in need – the sick and the poor, all those whose way through life is marked by pain, anxiety, and acute hardship . . . Teach us, Lord, that the qualities of love and compassion are one and the same, that the largest obligation of our discipleship is to share these gifts with those who need them.

For those who have died:

We pray for those who have died, those who have completed the way of the world and now live in the peace of the spirit . . . The message of resurrection is that God's love is supreme and irrefutable. Open our hearts that this assurance of hope and redemption may be heard and reflected in our lives.

Finally . . .

Rejoicing in the fellowship of (N and of) all your saints, we commend ourselves and all Christian people to your unfailing love.

The Fruit of the Spirit

For the Church:

> We offer prayers for the Church, God's tree of love planted in the world to yield spiritual fruit ... Lord, the Church is a constant reminder to us of the difference between earthly and spiritual values, the contrast between the world of human ambitions and the kingdom of God's peace. Guide your Church, that its members may always distinguish clearly between the voice of temptation and that of their Lord.

For the world:

> We pray for nations in the pursuit of worldly supremacy, governments who would rule the world and possess its riches without regard for the spiritual and moral destruction they may cause. We pray for leaders so obsessed with their own egotistical interpretation of the world and its destiny, that they would sacrifice the lives and welfare of their people in the pursuit of personal power. Into such a world come, Lord, with the still small voice of your love, compassion, and humility.

For the local community:

> We pray for our (village, town, etc.), especially for those whose concern is the spiritual and

psychological health of its citizens ... Teach us, Lord, that the material prosperity of our community is meaningless without a spiritual dimension to give it purpose and direction, that without the spirit of love and mutual concern, all of our material wealth becomes but the empty result of selfish ambition.

For those in need:

We pray for those in need – for those who are ill, frightened, and spiritually impoverished, those without a faith to sustain them in the crisis of their lives ... May your spirit of healing and reconciliation be planted in their hearts and bear fruit in the increased health of their confidence and self-esteem.

For those who have died:

We remember those who have died and have shared in the spiritual harvest of resurrection and eternal rest ... Having given fully of their talents in the world, may they now enjoy the dividends of their faithfulness in the spiritual life to which you have called them.

Finally ...

Rejoicing in the fellowship of (N and of) all your saints, we commend ourselves and all Christian people to your unfailing love.

The Whole Armour of God

For the Church:

> We offer prayers for your Church and its leaders.
> We recognize the Church as a small remnant of
> faith in a world largely ambivalent towards its
> principles. The gospel of love and peace rings
> hollow in the ears of worldly and self-centred
> ambition. Give to your living body a new voice,
> a more creative imagination to preach you more
> emphatically and persuasively in the face of
> scepticism and indifference.

For the world:

> We pray for a world whose armour is not God,
> but rather the armaments of destruction and
> annihilation, nations who take refuge and security
> in the blatant acquisition of power rather than the
> service of their people . . . Lord, teach those in
> authority that they have within themselves
> resources of spiritual and moral strength which
> they ignore and pervert to their peril and to their
> eternal cost. Put into their leadership a strong
> dynamic of humility and concern for the good of
> your whole creation.

For the local community:

> Lord, we offer you our local community as it
> struggles to assert itself and be recognized within
> the context of society at large. How often the

local authority is regarded with polite indifference by the state; how frequently the talents and gifts of local officials are lost in the sea of big government. Lord, give your blessing to our towns and villages, that our individual rights and opinions may be respected.

For those in need:

We pray for those in need – the sick, the poor, and especially those who are weak and helpless in the face of aggressive power and authority . . . Comfort them, Lord, with a reminder that your Son was physically vulnerable to the brutality of temporal power, that he subjected himself meekly to the torments and injuries which he suffered at the hands of cruel men, but that by virtue of his spiritual perfection and strength, he was not destroyed, rather he was invincible.

For those who have died:

We celebrate the memory of those who have died, those who by faith have won the final victory and have grasped the prize of eternal life . . . Help us to see, Lord, that in their resurrection with Christ, they have, on our behalf, overcome the fear of death, and have exposed it as but a minor irritant on the way to glory in Christ's eternal presence. Eternal rest etc.

Finally . . .

Rejoicing in the fellowship (*N* and of) all your saints, we commend ourselves and all Christian people to your unfailing love.

all adversities which may happen to the body as for all evil thoughts which may assault as hurt the soul through Jesus Christ our Lord.

The Mind of Christ

For the Church:

> We offer prayers for your Church and its leaders,
> that living body of your Son in which the mind
> of Christ is alive and at work ... It is all too easy
> for the Church to take itself so seriously, to
> assess its authority and mission so personally,
> that it becomes more a hindrance than a help to
> your direct and active witness in the world. Fill
> the Church with a spirit of humility and self-
> effacement, that in its ministry your divine and
> eternal presence may be clearly discerned.

For the world:

> We pray for a world torn by conflict and greed,
> nations unwilling to share their respective assets
> with others, governments contemptuous of
> Christ's call to humility and the sharing of
> material and spiritual resources ... We pray that
> you would reveal your mind, your love, your
> will, to your wayward creation, that it may know
> and serve you in the spirit of mutual tolerance,
> concern, and reconciliation.

For the local community:

> We offer you our community with all its tensions
> and prejudices. We know that prejudice and
> intolerance are often most virulent and visible in
> small communities, and that they run counter to

the mind of Christ which demands unconditional mutual love and tolerance. Lord, make us immune to racial and cultural hatred, that we may truly love our neighbour for his humanity alone, and thereby help to heal the social fabric of our community.

For those in need:

We pray for those in need – for the arrogant, the proud, and all those whose egocentric lives cut them off from the mind of Christ. We pray for those who are unable to confess their own fallibility, and are thus blind to Christ's forgiveness, those to whom Christ's mind and love is irrelevant because it is rejected . . . Teach them, Lord, that you help and heal those who, to at least some extent, help themselves, those who co-operate with your will to mend and integrate their broken lives.

For those who have died:

We pray for those who have died, those who are completely in tune with the mind of Christ as it motivates life in your kingdom . . . May we, whose vision of your will is now obscured and distorted by uncertainty, be sustained by renewed faith in a full and perfect perception of your love which is to come.

Finally . . .

Rejoicing in the fellowship (N and of) all your saints, we commend ourselves and all Christian people to your unfailing love.

The Serving Community

For the Church:

We offer prayers for the Church and its leaders,
the community of witnesses called upon to serve
you in the world . . . We confess a certain
complacency that belies our vulnerability to
scepticism and hostility. Remind us, Lord, that to
preach Christ can be a lonely vocation inviting
the ridicule and rejection of the world, but that
such service has its reward in the strength and
courage which Christ supplies to the faithful.

For the world:

We pray for a world in turmoil, for nations in
conflict, for leaders headstrong in their lust for
power . . . Lord, remind those with secular power
and authority that they are elected to serve more
than dominate, that true service is at heart
statesmanship, and that statesmanship is
characterized by genuine compassion and concern
for the common welfare, a firm commitment to
the promotion of justice, enlightenment, and
freedom.

For the local community:

We lay before you our local community and its
elected officials . . . We pray especially for our
service industries, organized to enhance and

enrich the quality and effectiveness of community life, our churches and other charitable institutions called upon to serve the spiritual and psychological needs of our people . . . May their service be self-effacing, so that the person and love of Christ may be perceived at the centre of their ministry.

For those in need:

We pray for the sick, the poor, and all those who in their suffering cry out to be healed . . . We pray especially for those whose vocation is to alleviate pain and lessen the burden of suffering and anxiety . . . May their service be Christlike in its selfless and untiring mission to reach out to the have-nots of society in a ministry of comfort, reassurance, and reconciliation.

For those who have died:

We celebrate the lives of those who have died in Christ, whose service in the world has been rewarded with a new and eternal life in the spiritual community of your kingdom . . . May our remaining time in the world be spent in the service of Christ, as we demonstrate his gospel of love to a sceptical and often indifferent world.

Finally . . .

Rejoicing in the fellowship of (N and of) all your saints, we commend ourselves and all Christian people to your unfailing love.

TWELFTH SUNDAY
AFTER PENTECOST
(Trinity 11)

The Witnessing Community

For the Church:

> We offer prayers for the Church, your living
> body of witness, called upon to preach Christ's
> reconciliation in a divided and intolerant world
> . . . As your community of faith, may the
> Church's message be one of hope, a firm
> declaration that in Christ all things, even the
> Church's own weaknesses and failings, are made
> new in the sight of God.

For the world:

> We pray for a world divided against itself,
> nations plagued by the dissonance of mutual
> suspicion and hatred, distrust and fear . . . Into
> this discord come with your balm of
> reconciliation, your harmony of love and mutual
> concern. Remind us, Lord, that just as you created
> us one undivided people, so must we strive to
> live in unity if we are to survive and prosper in
> the spirit of your sustaining power.

For the local community:

> We lay before you our community in which we
> bear witness to the social interdependence which
> binds us together. Make us always aware of the
> fact that community life is only as strong as the
> relationships of which it is comprised, and may

these relationships be sustained as an expression
of the spiritual ties which enable us to call you
'Our Father'.

For those in need:

We pray for those in need, those in whose hearts
and bodies suffering and anxiety create
disharmony and disease . . . Lord, teach us that
the suffering community is a very special one in
close relationship with your suffering Son. May
we discover in the vulnerability to pain a source
of our own humility and thankfulness.

For those who have died:

Let us remember those who have died, those who
have joined that vast community of saints who
bear witness to your resurrection and glory . . .
Let us pray that their peace may be eternal, and
that as they rejoice in a direct knowledge of their
Lord, so may we who now 'see through a glass
darkly' also reach the ultimate goal of our faith, a
clear vision of God's love.

Finally . . .

Rejoicing in the fellowship of (N and of) all your
saints, we commend ourselves and all Christian
people to your unfailing love.

The Suffering Community

For the Church:

> We offer prayers for the Church and its leaders
> . . . As we drift along in a Church which is
> generally accepted or at least tolerated, it is
> difficult to believe that the Christian community
> ever suffered the intense physical persecution of
> its early history. Our own worst enemy is
> complacency and cosiness, whereas that of the
> early Church was annihilation. Yet we are
> reminded that the Church's finest hour was that
> in which the strength of her faith was severely
> tested and found sufficient to sustain her in her
> suffering. Lord, make us uncomfortable.

For the world:

> We pray for a world steeped in suffering and
> death, nations in which countless families are
> homeless and visit the graves of loved ones,
> governments which exploit their people in the
> pursuit of power. Yet there is no dignity or
> nobility in the world's suffering because it is self-
> inflicted and deserved. Teach your creation, Lord,
> that the only meaningful suffering is that which is
> undeserved, suffering endured in the cause of
> freedom and liberation, suffering which looks to
> the welfare of the whole creation.

For the local community:

We offer you our local community, especially those who work to alleviate suffering in our midst . . . Make them aware of the responsibility they bear in their healing ministry, and the opportunity they enjoy to use their talents in the strengthening and enrichment of community life.

For those in need:

We pray for all those who are in need. All about us we observe pockets of suffering – marriages in trouble, estrangement between parents and children, the victims of ostracism and prejudice, the elderly who are neglected, the sick and the poor . . . Lord, give us the perception, the spirit of Christian love and compassion, to exercise Christ's ministry of healing and comfort in all of our relationships.

For those who have died:

We pray for those who have died, those whom death has liberated from their suffering and are now alive in Christ . . . For them the cross and passion are but a memory, the resurrection an eternal reality. We who follow them have yet to travel the narrow hard way of suffering which leads to eternity. May the faith of those who have gone before us strengthen us in our spiritual pilgrimage.

Finally . . .

Rejoicing in the fellowship (*N* and of) all your saints, we commend ourselves and all Christian people to your unfailing love.

FOURTEENTH SUNDAY AFTER PENTECOST
(Trinity 13)

The Family

For the Church:

> Lord, we lay before you the Church and its
> leaders, your spiritual family in the world . . . As
> the remnant of faith, it is the Church's mission to
> reach out and draw all of your children, even the
> most unlovable and rebellious, into the spiritual
> family circle. Remind us, Lord, that just as the
> human family is ever on the move, ever
> changing, so must the Church avoid stagnation
> and continually preach Christ in a manner that
> grips the soul of contemporary society and
> compels attention.

For the world:

> We pray for the family of man, broken and
> divided; for nations in conflict and disarray
> . . . Governments pay lip-service to the concepts
> of interdependence and mutual concern, while at
> the same time pursuing their own individual ends
> in their quest for global supremacy. We call you
> 'Father', Lord, yet we continually rebel against
> your authority. Because of pride and ambition in
> high places, the world stands in peril of oblivion,
> and so we pray for the spirit of contentment and
> humility, for the capacity and will to use our
> power and resources for the common good.

For the local community:

> We lay before you our local community and the
> family life which binds us together. Teach us,
> Lord, that our homes and families are but
> microcosms of that greater relationship with you
> in which we count ourselves your children and
> call you 'Father', that if, in our earthly families
> there is disharmony and conflict, so are there
> similar tensions in our spiritual relationship with
> you.

For those in need:

> We pray for those in need, especially those who
> live alone and without the support of family life.
> We pray for those who are homeless, families
> that have sacrificed husbands, wives, and children,
> to the hatred and slaughter of armed conflict.
> Visit them with the spirit of your compassion and
> comfort, that they may lose their bitterness as
> their lives are renewed.

For those who have died:

> We remember the departed, those who have
> joined the great family of God's faithful in his
> kingdom . . . We celebrate their lives of devotion
> to Christ, their faithful witness to his gospel, and
> we ask for your blessing as we strive to imitate
> Christ in the face of all the temptations which
> assail us.

Finally . . .

> Rejoicing in the fellowship of (N and of) all your
> saints, we commend ourselves and all Christian
> people to your unfailing love.

Those in Authority

For the Church:

> We offer you the Church, especially its ordained
> ministry . . . Bless them with the spirit of humility
> in the exercising of their authority. Make them
> acutely aware of their identity as the voice and
> presence of Christ in the world, all of their power
> and authority being his and his alone.

For the world:

> We pray for the governments of nations, for
> leaders elected to positions of secular authority
> and power. We pray especially for those who
> have misused their authority to repress and
> exploit their people, governments whose mandate
> to serve has been perverted into a mere licence to
> exercise personal ambition and power. Teach
> them, Lord, that secular authority must be but an
> extension of your will, that secular power, rightly
> used, must be an expression of your will to
> redeem the world.

For the local community:

> We offer you our community and its people,
> especially our local officials and the government
> which they comprise . . . Fill them with a sincere
> devotion to service, a genuine commitment to the

welfare of the community, and the spirit of your presence in all of their deliberations and decisions.

For those in need:

We pray for those in need, those who are sick, poor, and utterly dependent for their survival upon the good will of individuals and corporate charity ... May those with the authority and capacity to relieve suffering and anxiety realize that they do Christ's work in the world. May the instincts which motivate charity be the same as those which enabled Jesus to identify so closely with suffering, namely love, forgiveness, and compassion.

For those who have died:

We remember those who have died, those who have yielded to your ultimate authority to defeat death and create a new order of life for those who love you ... Recognizing the great privilege they enjoy in your gift of resurrection, may our faith be such that we are deemed worthy of sharing the new life which you offer.

Finally ...

Rejoicing in the fellowship of (N and of) all your saints, we commend ourselves and all Christian people to your unfailing love.

The Neighbour

For the Church:

> We pray for your Church, the living body of
> Christ summoned to love the world, to be its
> neighbour in compassion and faith, and to inspire
> neighbourliness in others . . . Strengthen your
> Church in its task of bringing love to the world,
> that the covenant which you have established
> with your creation may endure and flourish.

For the world:

> We offer you a world in which nations live close
> together, many of them with long common
> borders. Yet whereas close proximity should
> breed good neighbours and inspire mutual
> concern, instead it often plants the seeds of
> mutual suspicion and fear, producing the
> poisonous blossoms of conflict and war. Lord,
> create between cultures and nations a spirit of
> love and mutual tolerance, forces which must lie
> at the heart of peaceful and healthy relationships.

For the local community:

> We pray for our (village, town, etc.) with its rich
> diversity of relationships. We pray especially for
> those neighbourhoods in which relationships are
> poisoned by distrust and prejudice. Remind us,
> Lord, that productive and harmonious

neighbourhoods are the key to a vital and vigorous community, that families united by the spirit of love and charity are the foundation of communal prosperity.

For those in need:

We pray for those who are in need, those cut off from the mainstream of society and in need of love and acceptance. Lord, help us to be good neighbours to those who are alone, those in whom alienation has created despair and despondency.

For those who have died:

We celebrate the memory of those who have died, those who now know the perfect love and peace of your kingdom . . . Ever the perfect neighbour, you accept in love the whole of your creation, offering to them an eternal share in your resurrected life. May we accept your offer by responding to your love and putting you at the centre of our lives.

Finally . . .

Rejoicing in the fellowship of (*N* and of) all your saints, we commend ourselves and all Christian people to your unfailing love.

SEVENTEENTH SUNDAY AFTER PENTECOST

(Trinity 16)

The Proof of Faith

For the Church:

ministers

Lord, we offer prayers for the Church, its ~~clergy~~
and people . . . As the living body of your Son at
work in the world, the Church is living proof of
your faith in mankind's capacity to respond to
your love and be saved. May the Church's
witness be one of both word and action as she
embodies Christ in her ministry.

For the world:

We pray for a world in which many faithless
leaders wield power and authority, nations whose
security rests in the pursuit of dominance, and
whose governments have faith not in spiritual
riches, but in the mindless pursuit of material
wealth. Turn the hearts of all those in authority,
that they may see the world's ills in terms of a
broken spirit, and its healing in terms of Christ's
spirit of love and reconciliation.

For the local community:

We lay before you our local community and the
officials elected to represent our interests . . . How
often is the political promise at variance with the
political deed; how frequently the political
platform bears no resemblance to the policies
enacted. How easy are words, how difficult
corresponding actions. Teach our elected officials

that political posturing is an exercise in deception,
that commitment to service has meaning only in
terms of deeds which bring words to life.

For those in need:

> We pray for those in need, those whose illness
> and anxiety renders them vulnerable to despair,
> deprivation, and exploitation . . . Protect them
> from bitterness, Lord, with the gift of faith, an
> absolute trust in your love, concern, mercy, and
> power to heal.

For those who have died:

> We offer you the souls of those who have died,
> those whose faith has been proved in the risen
> life which they share with Christ . . . May a
> portion of their faith and trust be ours as we
> struggle to finish the race that is set before us.

Finally . . .

> Rejoicing in the fellowship of (N and of) all your
> saints, we commend ourselves and all Christian
> people to your unfailing love.

**EIGHTEENTH SUNDAY
AFTER PENTECOST**
(Trinity 17)

The Offering of Life

For the Church:

We pray for the Church, its clergy and people ...
As Christ's body in the world, the Church is
called upon to offer itself as a catalyst in the
world's spiritual growth and development.
Remind us, Lord, as individual witnesses to
Christ's love, that the strength of the Church's
offering depends entirely upon our own will to
offer time, tithes, and talent, to the support of its
life and ministry.

For the world:

We lay before you a world offered to us in all
the beauty and richness of your creating power, a
world which we, in turn, defile and desecrate in
the name of progress and the management of our
natural resources. Teach us Lord, that we are
stewards, not masters, of the earth, and that we
ignore this distinction to our peril. Remind us
that the ultimate sacrilege is to accept from you
the earth in all its life and beauty, and return it to
you a barren and lifeless wasteland.

For the local community:

We offer you our local community, and the many
individuals and institutions who offer resources
for its nourishment and growth ... Remind us

that whereas it is tempting to regard the community as a nameless and impersonal machine, it is, in truth, the sum total of personal needs and aspirations that comprises its life and vitality.

For those in need:

Lord, we pray for those in need, those without the health or resources to offer themselves in the service of your creation . . . Bless those who do the healing work of Christ with the perception to regard their vocation as one of assisting in the renewal of that life and vitality which God offers to all of his children.

For those who have died:

We pray for those who have died, those who have accepted your offer of eternal life and now live with you in your kingdom . . . We pray that we who follow them may be stewards of your gifts, serve you in love, and thereby join you in the peace of resurrection.

Finally . . .

Rejoicing in the fellowship of (N and of) all your saints, we commend ourselves and all Christian people to your unfailing love.

NINETEENTH SUNDAY AFTER PENTECOST

(Trinity 18)

The Life of Faith

For the Church:

> We offer prayers for the Church, called upon by you to follow the hard, narrow, and demanding way of Christ in the world ... Strengthen your living body, Lord, that however uncompromising the demands of your gospel, yet the Church's faith and commitment may be equal to the task at hand.

For the world:

> We pray for a world whose only faith is in its own accomplishments, nations committed to the principles of expansion and conquest, leaders whose lust for power consumes and destroys the weak and the vulnerable ... Raise up in this broken world leaders who are statesmen, whose commitment is to peaceful co-existence, whose trust is in the underlying brotherhood of man which binds us all together in the spirit of mutual support and reconciliation.

For the local community:

> We lay before you our (village, town, etc.), its homes and institutions. Create in local government a greater spirit of integrity, that we may shed our cynicism and have a greater faith in its policies and intentions. Make our officials more

responsive to the needs of the community, and less driven by the impulse of their selfish ambitions.

For those in need:

We pray for the sick and the poor, for the disadvantaged of our society, and for all who find the life of faith difficult and elusive. Having been repeatedly disillusioned, they receive all of the empty promises and gestures of charity with understandable bitterness and cynicism. Visit them, Lord, with your compassion and comfort, that they may find in you a faith in the possibility of new life, new opportunities, new beginnings.

For those who have died:

We pray for those who have died, those whose firm faith in Christ's promises has been rewarded in the life of resurrection . . . May we who remain discover in Christ's victory over death the basis of our own Easter faith and trust, the truth of Christ's assurance that where he has gone, we will surely follow.

Finally . . .

Rejoicing in the fellowship of (N and of) all your saints, we commend ourselves and all Christian people to your unfailing love.

Endurance

For the Church:

We pray for your Church and its leaders.
Especially for the Church in lands of oppression
and hostility who are called upon to endure
severe hardships in their ministry of faith, to
follow the hard and narrow way in the witness of
your kingdom . . . Surrounded by the seductive
power of worldly values, the temptation to
accommodate is overwhelming. Maintain in the
comportment of your Church a firm and clear
distinction between being in the world and being
of it.

For the world:

We lay before you a world caught in the grip of
conflict and suffering, a global community
bleeding from the self-inflicted wounds of greed
and oppression . . . For weak nations, those
without the capacity or resources to protect
themselves, the suffering becomes almost
unendurable. Lord, teach strong nations that the
survival of mankind depends utterly upon the
responsible and compassionate use of their power,
that their strength and authority must be
employed to heal, not intensify, the world's
suffering.

For the local community:

We pray for our community as it searches for its identity in relation to county and national government. Where there is conflict and suspicion, create harmony and peace, to the end that divisions may be healed, and that a bond of trust and faith may be established.

For those in need:

We offer prayers for those in need, those who are poor, hungry, and alone, who are sick and without the strength to endure . . . Liberate them, Lord, from the prison of their suffering, that they may know the Christ who heals, the Lord who promises new life at the end of their anguish, and that in Christ they may discover the capacity and will to endure.

For those who have died:

We celebrate the lives of those who have died, those who have endured to the end and been saved . . . For many of them life was not easy; they were subjected to great hardships and severe tests of faith. And we pray that when our times of testing come, we may not be found wanting in courage, steadfastness, and endurance.

Finally . . .

Rejoicing in the fellowship of (N and of) all your saints, we commend ourselves and all Christian people to your unfailing love.

129

TWENTY-FIRST SUNDAY AFTER PENTECOST

(Trinity 20)

The Christian Hope

For the Church:

> We lay before you the Church, your community of hope in the world. We pray for clergy and people as they strive to demonstrate in their lives Christ's promise of redemption and forgiveness . . . Bless your disciples with the perception to demonstrate Christ's hope and optimism at the heart of what is often a discouraging and disheartening ministry of his love.

For the world:

> We pray for a world riddled with hopelessness and despair – a world composed of rich and poor nations – the former arrogant and self-centred, the latter weak and consumed by poverty and starvation. Lord, teach the affluent and the impoverished of this world that they need each other, that from the poor the rich may learn humility, and that from the rich the poor may have access to the resources which may relieve their suffering and instil hope where once there was only despair.

For the local community:

> We offer prayers for our local community and its importance as the focus for all the hopes and aspirations of its people . . . Lord, raise leaders

who perceive the community not as a corporate machine, but rather as a group of individuals, each with his or her own needs and aspirations.

For those in need:

We pray for those who are in need, for the poor, the sick, and especially those who are terminally ill and waiting to die . . . Remind them that whereas there is little, if any, hope in this world, Christ's promise of life beyond death is strong and abiding.

For those who have died:

And now we remember the souls of those who have died, those whose hope and trust in Christ's promise of eternal life to the faithful has been justified . . . Just as it was a firm and abiding optimism in the essential goodness of life that sustained them in the world, so may we share in this optimism as we look to Christ for our support in adversity and our hope in the world to come.

Finally . . .

Rejoicing in the fellowship of (N and of) all your saints, we commend ourselves and all Christian people to your unfailing love.

The Two Ways

For the Church:

> We pray for the Church and its leaders, for those
> who have turned to Christ and made the
> fundamental decision to change their lives
> accordingly . . . The life of witness entails many
> moments of crisis and decision making, choices
> which often give pain and hardship precedence
> over pleasure and comfort, but which always
> place Christ and his principles at the centre of life.
> Strengthen us, Lord, in the decisions that we must
> make.

For the world:

> We pray for a world in crisis, nations backed into
> a corner and faced with life or death decisions.
> Governments who now possess uncontrollable
> forces must choose either the way of negotiation
> and reconciliation which is life, or the selfish
> pursuit of power and brutal domination which is
> death. Be present, Lord, in the decisions which
> they make.

For the local community:

> We pray for our (village, town, etc.), its families
> and individuals. Often the most important
> decisions that we make are in conjunction with
> the election of our leadership. Give wisdom to

our choices, and give us the strength of purpose to demand the best from those chosen to serve.

For those in need:

We lay before you those who suffer and are in pain – those who are in need of confidence and encouragement, who are lonely and frightened . . . Often they must choose between bitterness and forbearance, between hope and despair. Be with them, Lord, that they may make decisions which contribute to the restoration of health and personal welfare.

For those who have died:

We pray for those who have died, for the souls of those whose hope was in their Lord, and whose rest is now with him . . . The Christian hope is our Easter faith, our trust that by Christ's resurrection, we may follow him into his kingdom.

Finally . . .

Rejoicing in the fellowship of (*N* and of) all your saints, we commend ourselves and all Christian people to your unfailing love.

Citizens of Heaven

For the Church:

> Lord, we offer prayers for your Church and its
> ministry, a prophetic ministry which bears witness
> to the joy of your kingdom . . . Fill your Church
> with the vision and inspiration to portray the
> love and peace of Christ as a clear and
> compelling alternative to the hostility, conflict,
> and indifference that surround her.

For the world:

> We pray for the world that has lost its vision,
> nations blinded by their obsession with immediate
> and short-term ambition. In their pursuit of
> power, the world's leaders create conflict and the
> potential for global catastrophe. Lord, we pray for
> sanity and creative leadership in the corridors of
> power, for the bond of brotherhood, the desire
> for peaceful co-existence in the relationships
> between nations. Visit your creation with the
> spirit of reconciliation, that peace on earth may
> foreshadow the peace and harmony of your
> kingdom.

For the local community:

> We pray for our (village, town, etc.) and its
> people. We pray especially that our community
> may be a source of security, prosperity, and

happiness for all of us, that it may be a pleasant and happy place in which to live and work, thereby affording us a glimpse, a foretaste, of life in your kingdom.

For those in need:

We lay before you the sick and the poor, those in need of sustenance and the will to live . . . Visit them with the spirit of patience and hope; above all, bless them with a trustful and positive attitude toward their affliction, that they may know your presence, and accept suffering in the context of a strong faith in your will to heal and to comfort.

For those who have died:

We remember those who have died, those who have become full citizens of your kingdom . . . Just as in this world they strove to be perfect in faith, so may we follow their example. And just as they have received the prize of resurrection and life in your presence, so may we be found worthy to be reunited with them in your kingdom.

Finally . . .

Rejoicing in the fellowship of (N and of) all your saints, we commend ourselves and all Christian people to your unfailing love.